FINDING OUT ABOUT

Packaging

Contents

This edition published 1990 by
Franklin Watts
96 Leonard Street
London EC2A 4RH

ISBN 0 7496 0326 7

Original edition published 1988 by
Hobsons Publishing plc
Produced in conjunction with the
Industry Council for Packaging
and the Environment and
sponsored by the Coca-Cola
organisation in Great Britain, ICI plc
and Wimpy International

A CIP catalogue record for this book is
available from the British Library

Acknowledgements

We would like to thank the following for supplying photographic
and illustrative material:

Batchelors Foods Limited
BBC Hulton Picture Library
Birds Eye Walls' Ltd
The British Glass Manufacturers Confederation
The British Printing Industries Federation
The Can Makers Information Service
The Coca-Cola organisation in Great Britain
Corgi Toys Ltd
Creative Packaging Solutions Ltd
Goldenlay Eggs Limited
H J Heinz Company Ltd
ICI plc
INCPEN
Johnsen & Jorgensen Plastics Limited
The Keystone Collection
Lawson Marden Group
   (companies operating in the UK)
Metal Box
Milk Marketing Board
Reckitt & Colman
The Robert Opie Collection
J Sainsbury plc
Tetra Pak Limited
UK Corrugated
United Biscuits
Wimpy International

FINDING OUT ABOUT

Packaging

FRANKLIN WATTS
LONDON • NEW YORK • SYDNEY • TORONTO

What is packaging?

Most of the food we eat comes out of a pack. It could be a packet of cornflakes. It might be a can of baked beans, a frozen pizza, a pot of cream, a bottle of tomato sauce, a can of fizzy drink, a bag of potatoes, or a carton of ice cream.

And packaging is not only used for food – most of the things we buy in the shops come in some kind of package. It could be a new television in a strong case, a pack of cards, a box of tissues, a bottle of shampoo . . . or any one of thousands of purchases. Stop for a moment to think of things we buy that don't have any packaging. What do you think our lives would be like without packaging.

You've probably not given packaging much of a thought, either as an industry or as a product. And yet the evidence of it is all around you, especially when you go into a supermarket and see cans, cartons, tubes, plastic packs, bottles, jars, sacks and foil packets.

Packaging is an exciting industry because it matches clever design to modern technology. It's also important because it creates jobs for many people, it provides a vital service to protect, preserve and display goods of all kinds, and it creates business on which we all depend for our economy.

WHAT YOU CAN DO

To get started, look at these pictures.

1 Make a list of products that are packaged.

2 Write a list of the different kinds of special protection these products need.
For example, does the product break easily, does it go rotten, does it dry out, lose its flavour, go soggy? If it was left loose and insecure, would it damage other things? Can you think of any other problems?

3 Look at the pictures again. How do you know what's in the pack? Is it done by a 'window' or drawing or photograph and words?

How do you know what to do with it?

Packaging...and the consumer

The consumer is *you*. Packaging is important for all of us because it affects our lives in so many ways.

For example....

1 In years gone by, milk was delivered in milk churns to people's doors and to shops where it was ladled into jugs.

Result? Food poisoning causing sickness and diarrhoea.

2 In the past, shopkeepers used to weigh goods on scales; some cheated by keeping their finger on one of the balances.

Now? By law, the quantity of the product is printed on the pack.

3 Food used to be displayed unwrapped in shops, where insects and flies could get on to it.

Now, food is protected by packaging.

4 Today, people want convenience food that can be bought 'off the shelf' to be easily and quickly cooked and eaten at times that suit them.

So? We can get 'fast' service, and 'fast' cooking by means of modern packaging . . . and without a lot of washing-up.

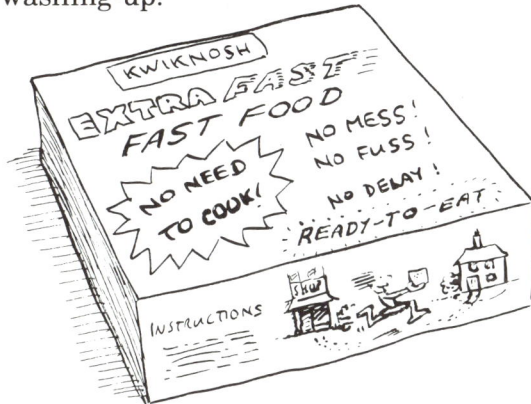

5 'How do you use this?' 'How many minutes do you need to cook it?' These are the questions that consumers ask. However, these days you don't have shop assistants to tell you, (and part of their wages would be added to the price of the food). Instead, the answer is on the label and there are diagrams to explain what to do.

6 Years ago, people could only buy foods that were in season. Now we can have produce such as peas, and strawberries all the year round. We can also enjoy a much greater variety of foods such as exotic fruits like pineapples and mangoes from far away countries.

These are some of the ways in which packaging can help consumers. But there are many other ways in which packaging has changed people's lives over the last 50 years. We are going to look at them. First, let's ask the main question – why package goods, anyway?

Why package?

There are four main reasons for packaging. These pictures illustrate them. What would you say are the four reasons?

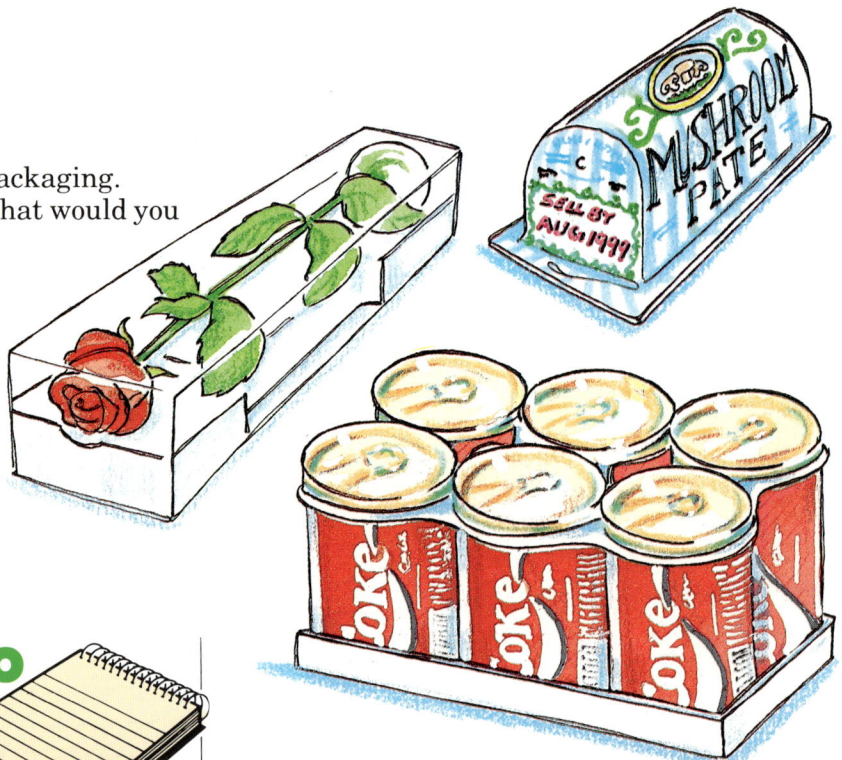

WHAT YOU CAN DO

To help you to work out the answers, let's look at the same question another way. Here are four manufacturing problems involving packaging. Suppose you are the manager in charge. How would you solve the problems?

1 You are the manager of a factory that cans or freezes peas. How do you handle them? Vegetables start losing their nutrient value as soon as they are picked. How can you make sure that they are sold in as fresh a condition as possible?

2 You are the manager of a soft drinks packing line. How are you going to get the bottles safely, without damage, to the wholesaler's warehouse?

3 You are the manager of a pharmaceuticals factory producing medicines such as tablets, cough mixtures, and inhalers for asthma sufferers. It is important that people take the right amount of the medicine at the right time. How can packaging help them?

4 You are the manager of a factory which makes 50,000 packs of different cheeses every week. Your job is to package them so that they are delivered safely and without damage of any kind to 2,000 shops and without the smell of Stilton being transferred to Cheddar! What problems does this present for you?

Write the answers to these four questions in your notebook and talk about your solutions with your friends.

The purposes of packaging

By looking at the four pictures on the previous page and by thinking about the managers' problems, you might have decided on the four main reasons for packaging:

1 To *preserve* food.

2 To *contain* objects so that they can be transported safely.

3 To *describe and identify* the contents so that customers know what it is, what its contents are, its weight, how they can use it, and any special instructions.

DISPRIN®

Disprin is taken in solution, so it is absorbed into the bloodstream faster than solid tablets. It is ready to tackle your pain fast.
For the relief of headache, toothache, neuralgia, period pains, rheumatic pain, lumbago and sciatica. To relieve the symptoms of influenza, feverishness, feverish colds and ease sore throats.

DIRECTIONS: Dissolve in water before taking.

DOSE: Adults and children over 12 yrs. 1-3 tablets (maximum 13 tablets in 24 hours). The dose may be repeated after 4 hours but the maximum dose in 24 hours must not be exceeded.
If symptoms persist consult your doctor.

DO NOT GIVE TO CHILDREN UNDER 12 UNLESS YOUR DOCTOR TELLS YOU TO

Children under 12 years should be given Junior Disprol which contains paracetamol in soluble tablets and sugar-free suspension.

KEEP OUT OF REACH OF CHILDREN

CONTAINS ASPIRIN

EACH DISPRIN TABLET CONTAINS 300mg ASPIRIN BP
SAFETY-WRAPPED IN FOIL

Made in Britain
Reckitt & Colman
Pharmaceutical Division, Hull
Export Distributors,   HK–06643
Reckitt & Colman (Overseas) Ltd, Hull
Printed in Britain   PL 44/5001

4 To *protect* the contents so that the goods arrive without damage or spoilage.

As you will learn later, there is a fifth important reason for packaging, which is sales and marketing.

Times are changing

Packaging methods have adapted over the years as people's lifestyles have changed.

1 **Food** — everyone's basic necessity – must be functionally packed to stop it going rotten and make sure it is sold hygienically and conveniently. People also expect to see more variety and food from different countries in the shops.

2 In recent years, people's **eating habits** have changed. Some families still sit down to eat together. But many families don't. If everyone in the family is eating something different at different times, it's easier to prepare quick meals or snacks – and at a time that suits them and no one else. Nowadays, food is often packaged as quick meals for one or two people.

3 Then there's the 'freezer and microwave revolution'. People expect food to be packaged to suit fridges, freezers, microwave ovens, toasters and high pressure cookers.

4 **'Healthy eating'** is becoming more popular as people realise the importance of a balanced diet. As a result, food manufacturing companies have introduced low-fat foods and ready-made vegetarian dishes.

5 Far more women go out to work now than before. Families need foods that can be prepared quickly if there isn't someone at home doing the cooking.

6 **Competition** is keener than ever before. Companies that sell the same product such as drinks, food, clothes, games have to catch the eye of customers. So they use advertising, and colourful labels and packs.

7 **Leisure** is another important influence. People are buying more electronic goods such as televisions, hi-fi equipment, radios and videos and so manufacturers have had to make their packaging strong enough to withstand distribution. (For example, until recently, up to 25% of goods like televisions and videos were damaged in transit because of inadequate packaging.)

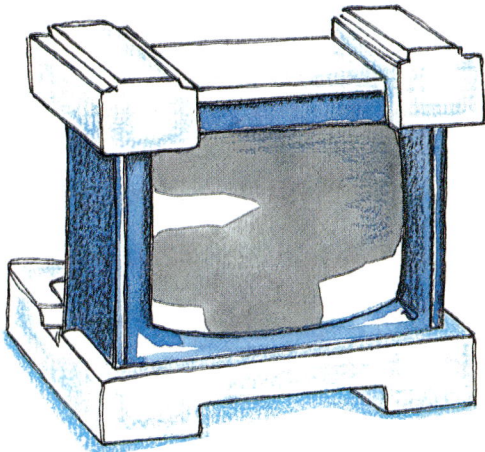

8 The general **standard of living** is higher than it was twenty years ago. People are therefore able to spend more money on clothes, food, household goods and so on, and expect higher standards than before.

Modern packaging has adapted to these changes:

- Fresh food such as vegetables and fruit can be frozen, chilled and stored in order to be eaten 'out of season', that is all the year round.

- Food that is popular in other countries – such as pizzas, paella, yoghurts and many more – can be on sale in the restaurants, cafes and shops of Britain, without having to go to Italy, Spain or Norway to enjoy them. British products like whisky and marmalade are sold all over the world. Nowadays, British companies even make pizzas that are sold in Italy!

- Light affects some foods and destroys their nutritional value. With modern packaging this can be prevented. For example, wine, beer and other drinks are often packaged in dark containers to preserve their taste.

- We are all becoming more aware of how important it is to conserve energy and resources for future generations, and to make the best use of materials such as paper, plastics, glass and metals. The packaging industry uses the smallest amount of material that will do the job properly.

9

WHAT YOU CAN DO

Collect cartons, cans or other kinds of packaging, or cut out pictures from magazines to illustrate these examples:

1 Fresh food (lettuce, oranges)

2 'Convenience' foods (pizzas, stuffed jacket potatoes)

3 **Ready-to-eat foods (hamburgers and chips, yoghurt, salads, crisps)**

4 **Fizzy drinks (cola)**

5 Non-fizzy drinks (orange juice, milk)

6 Fragile food (eggs)

7 Toiletries (toothpaste, hair gel)

8 Meats (bacon, sausages, chops)

9 Protective packaging (video tapes, computers, televisions)

10 Household cleaners (furniture polish, bleach)

11 Frozen foods (peas, fish fingers)

12 Garden products where safety is important

13 Bulky, awkward to handle products (flour, sugar, coffee granules)

For each of your examples and illustrations, write a few lines to describe a) the product; b) what type of packaging you think would protect it.

In your group, discuss whether you think these methods of packaging work. Can you think of other ways of packaging each of your examples?

2 Shopping in the good old days ... or were they really good?

Years ago, food was sold in shops like the one in the picture. Different foods were stored in sacks and drums, and the amount the customer wanted was ladled out into shopping bags or boxes to be carried home.

In some parts of the world, food is still displayed like this in markets and on the streets. In your class or group, discuss the problems of handling and packaging food in this way.

Here's a picture of another shop, years ago. What do you notice about it?

Discuss the way the food in the picture is
- protected and preserved
- advertised
- displayed
- weighed and measured
- priced
- what foods were available.

Suppose a customer comes along to buy butter, cheese, bread, eggs, sugar, bacon, tea and meat from this shop (they are all in the photograph). How would these goods have been wrapped and taken away from this shop, 80 years ago? Can you think of anything you wouldn't have been able to buy from this food shop? You could ask older people about how food was packaged and sold years ago. There are also some books listed on page 47 which will help you think about it.

Even today, some shops have their goods on open shelves, ready for customers to choose. For example, some sweet shops have toffees, sweets and chocolates on the counter or in large boxes and you – the customer – can weigh the amount of sweets you want and put them in a paper bag to take away. There's nothing wrong with that. Or is there? Are there any problems in selling unwrapped chocolate and sweets from open shelves? Is there a danger, or isn't there? And if there is, how do you think people in tropical countries survive, when all the fruit, meat and other food is unwrapped and could be contaminated (made bad) by dust, people's dirty fingers, insects, etc? Find out about the problems of food packaging in tropical countries and write a paragraph about it.

Today, in this country, very little food is wasted. In developing countries about one-third is wasted. It goes rotten or is damaged because of the lack of proper storage, distribution and packaging.

WHAT YOU CAN DO

Write three lists of a) ways in which food can be damaged or go bad if it isn't protected; b) ways of protecting food; and c) ways of preserving food. Set out your answer like this:

Causes of damage to food

1 ....
2 ....
3 ....

Ways of protecting food

1 ....
2 ....
3 ....

Ways of preserving food

1 ....
2 ....
3 ....

Shopping in your grandmother's day ... and today

As you can see, 80 years ago most grocers sold small amounts and packaged their goods in the shop itself. Sugar was dug out of a sack. Butter was sliced from a large slab. Bacon was cut on a slicing machine.

When people bought these goods, each purchase was wrapped separately in paper. All the shopkeeper needed was a large supply of greaseproof paper, paper bags and string. The customer needed a lot of patience because it took time to wait to be served, then to ask for each item – meat, cheese, butter, watch them being weighed, and then being parcelled up, ready for the shopping bag.

Shopkeepers used to collect the food themselves from local farmers or small local factories. Not much food was imported from other countries.

Today, shopping is very different. In the first place, your grandmother probably visited six different shops to buy bread, butter, toothpaste, vegetables, meat and a bottle-opener. She had to shop every day because food did not keep longer than a day or two. Nowadays, all of these goods and hundreds more can be bought in one shop –

the supermarket. Even so, the six little shops still survive in many towns and villages. Some people simply like the personal service and the 'specialities' of a cheese shop, a delicatessen, – others can't carry a lot of shopping at once because they are old or don't have a car.

These changes in the way people shop have led to many changes in the way things are packaged, too. Goods are made in large quantities in a few big factories or produced in large quantities by farmers and then transported all over the country – and often to other countries. Today, many articles sold in a supermarket are packaged separately. Flour, sugar, sliced bread, bacon, margarine, light bulbs, pizzas, soap powder – they are all packaged in plastic bags or boxes, packets, glass bottles, shrink-wrapped film coverings or cans. And they are all on open shelves so that the customer chooses, selecting what he or she wants, checking the price and the 'sell by' date, and carrying them in a basket or in a trolley to a check-out. Shop assistants are now no longer expected to know all about the product they sell and how to use it – packaging does that for us today. Prices are different too: many things that are now cheap enough for most of us to be able to afford were luxuries in our grandmothers' day.

WHAT YOU CAN DO

1 Interview older people about shopping and shops 50 or so years ago. Do they prefer shops of today? If not, can they tell you why?
You could record these conversations on a cassette recorder. Or as a group you could prepare a questionnaire to be used at the interviews.

2 Make a list of the differences in packaging that older people have seen over the last 50 years and also list the things (mainly food) you *couldn't* have if we didn't have modern packaging techniques.

13

Early packaging

There's always been some kind of packaging. When Stone Age man killed a wild animal and carried it home to his campfire to share with his family, he probably wrapped the meat in a skin or in leaves to protect it from insects, the sun or the rain.

Since earliest times, people have stored away as much food as possible to last them through the winter, a harvest failure or some other crisis. Some of the earliest methods such as drying wheat in the sun and storing it away, smoking fish or storing meat in salt to make it last have been in existence for 2,000 years and are still used today. Glass blowing was developed around 1500 BC and bottles, jars and drinking vessels have been found in Roman sites. But, in spite of people's early efforts to protect and preserve their food, meat still rotted and corn went mouldy. To disguise the horrid taste and smell, people used spices and herbs in their cooking.

It is said that the first man to invent refrigeration was an Englishman, Francis Bacon in 1626. However, unfortunately he died while testing his theory – he caught a chill while gathering snow. About 200 years later, people dug pits in the ground and lined them with ice but this scheme didn't work too well in a heatwave.

In 1795, Napoleon offered a prize for anyone who could suggest a method of preserving food. A chef, Nicholas Appert, used sealed containers and glass bottles. This was the beginning of the canning industry. Appert used glass bottles and jars with corks to preserve meat, vegetables and fruit. An English inventor, Bryan Donkin, used metal (iron) plates which were dipped into tin (to protect them against rust) and then soldered to make a container. So the 'can' was born. The name does not come from the USA, as many people think, but from the old word 'tin-canister'. Cans of food were carried into battle in the Crimean War in 1854 and in 1910 Captain Scott took cans on his expedition to the Antarctic.

14

Over 150 years ago, then, people could buy peas, sardines and tomatoes in cans. However, they were disappointed by the weight – the cans were so heavy that they had to be taken home in a wheelbarrow, and often had to be opened with a hammer and chisel!

In Britain, fruit canning as a major industry started about 90 years ago but it was not until about 1930 that food in cans became part of everyday life. In the Second World War, food shortages meant that canned food was essential, both for soldiers at the front and for the people at home. Bottles were used too, and today, glass bottles are used for some foods which aren't suitable for cans or other containers.

One of the criticisms of canned or bottled food is that 'it isn't fresh'. But the only truly fresh food you eat is from the garden. Most food we eat has been picked or processed some time ago, transported and stored. Canned and bottled food, however, is picked, processed, sorted and canned in a matter of hours. No additives are needed to preserve it, because it is heated to a high enough temperature to kill off any bacteria that could cause the food to rot.

Paper and board containers also have a long history. Paper has been used as wrapping for centuries. Box-making for chocolates, biscuits, cakes – all kinds of different goods – was a major industry well over a hundred years ago.

Plastics are the most recently developed materials. One of the first plastics for packaging was discovered by the company ICI in 1933 by accident during an experiment with ethylene. Early plastics were made from coal but today most are made from oil.

WHAT YOU CAN DO

Write these sentences into your notebook, completing each one.

1 Nicholas Appert invented

....

2 Before we had packaging, food was preserved by

....

3 Among foods that are in glass bottles are

....

....

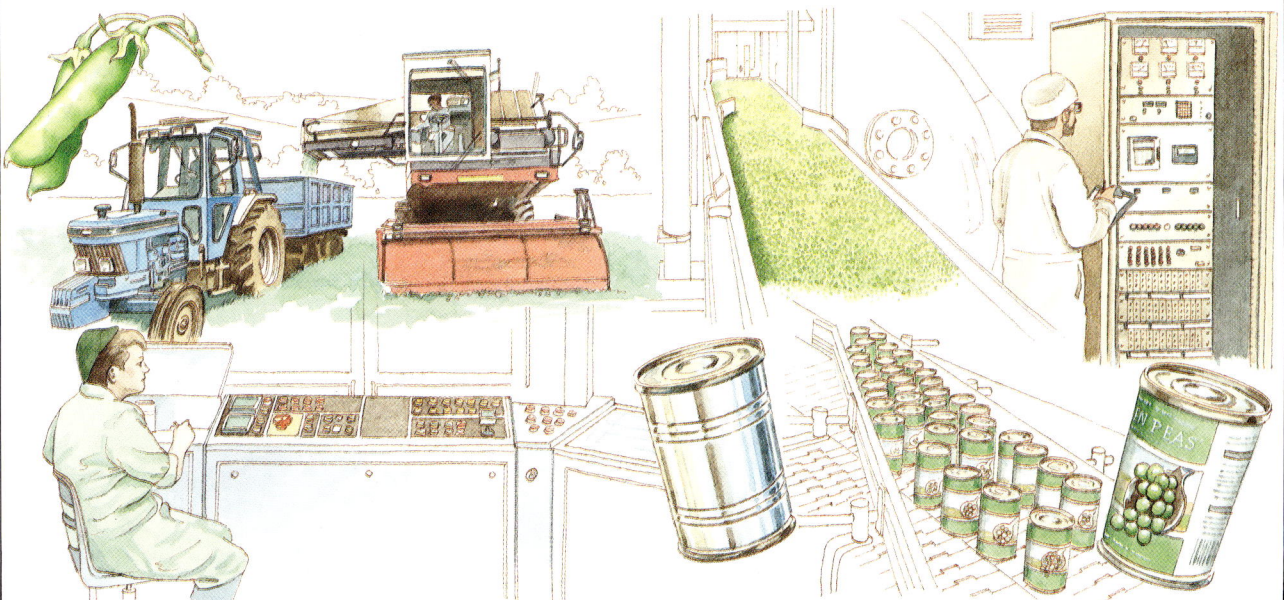

This pie-chart shows the different uses for packaging in the UK.

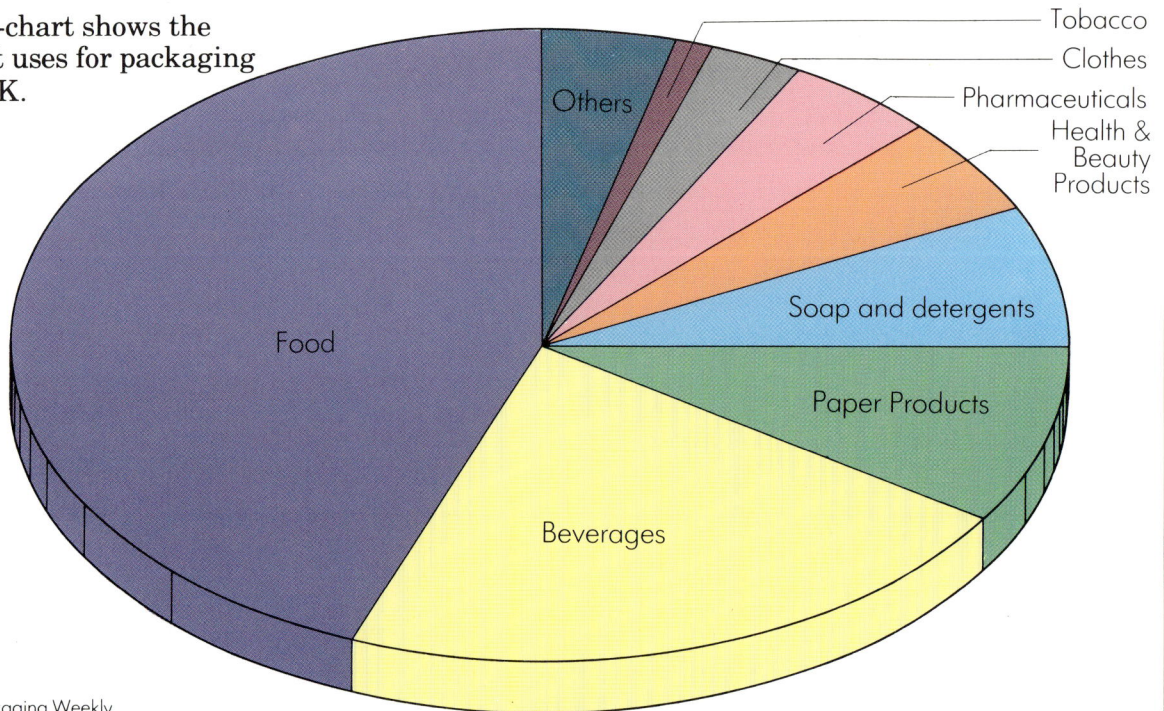

Food
Others
Beverages
Paper Products
Soap and detergents
Tobacco
Clothes
Pharmaceuticals
Health & Beauty Products

Source: Packaging Weekly

Consumption of Packaging Materials

(in kilograms per head of population, 1985)

	Europe	USA	Japan
Plastics	16	21	19
Paper and Board	38	100	80
Aluminium	1	5	17
Tinplate	11	15	
Glass	39	59	18
TOTAL	105	200	134

Europe

USA

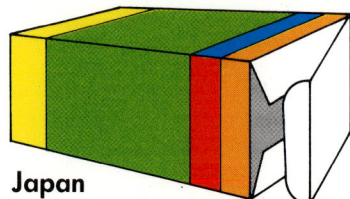

Japan

Source: Based on figures supplied by Mme Pardos, Pardos Marketing

WHAT YOU CAN DO

1 Look at the section for the food industry in the chart above. How much of the total packaging produced in the UK do you think it uses – 10%, 40%, 50%, 60%, or 80%?

2 Put the other types of industries (beverages, clothes, etc) into order from 1 for the biggest to 8 for the smallest. Estimate the percentage of the total for each of them.

What materials do we use?

The table shows the amount of packaging materials used in Europe, the USA and Japan. That means the amount of materials used in kilograms per head of the population in one year, 1985.

WHAT YOU CAN DO

1 In which country are more packaging materials used per person? Can you explain why?

2 Notice how much paper and board each person in the USA used compared with Europe. Why do you think this might be?

3 Why do you think people in Japan use more packaging materials than people in western Europe?

Plastics

We use plastics in nearly everything we do, often without realising it. At home, clothes, carpets, baths and brushes are often made of plastics. So too are parts of fridges and freezers, vacuum cleaners and washing machines. Modern houses have plastic guttering and downpipes; the connections to water and gas mains are made of plastic piping. Electrical wiring is insulated with a plastic covering.

Heart valves and false teeth are made of plastics. So are records and video tapes, compact discs and camera film. More than a thousand plastics parts are built into the average European car.

Where do plastics come from?

The first plastic, celluloid, was made from coal and used for billiard balls to avoid using ivory from elephants' tusks. Nowadays, only table tennis balls are made from celluloid.

Oil is used nowadays to make plastics, but less than 2% of the oil we use in this country is used to make plastics for packaging.

Plastics for packaging

Packaging plastics are produced in chemical factories and have rather long names. The six major ones are –

LDPE low density polyethylene
HDPE high density polyethylene
PP polypropylene
PVC polyvinylchloride
PS polystyrene
PET polyester (polyethylene terephthalate, try saying that if you are not a chemist!)

Luckily, they are usually known by their initials.

The plastics raw materials (called polymers) usually come in granule or powder form. They are then converted by companies called converters, who use heat and pressure on special processing machinery to produce bottles, tubs and films.

Thirty years ago plastic bottles used to look cloudy and we could easily distinguish them from glass bottles. But scientists have now learnt how to stretch plastics in a special way to

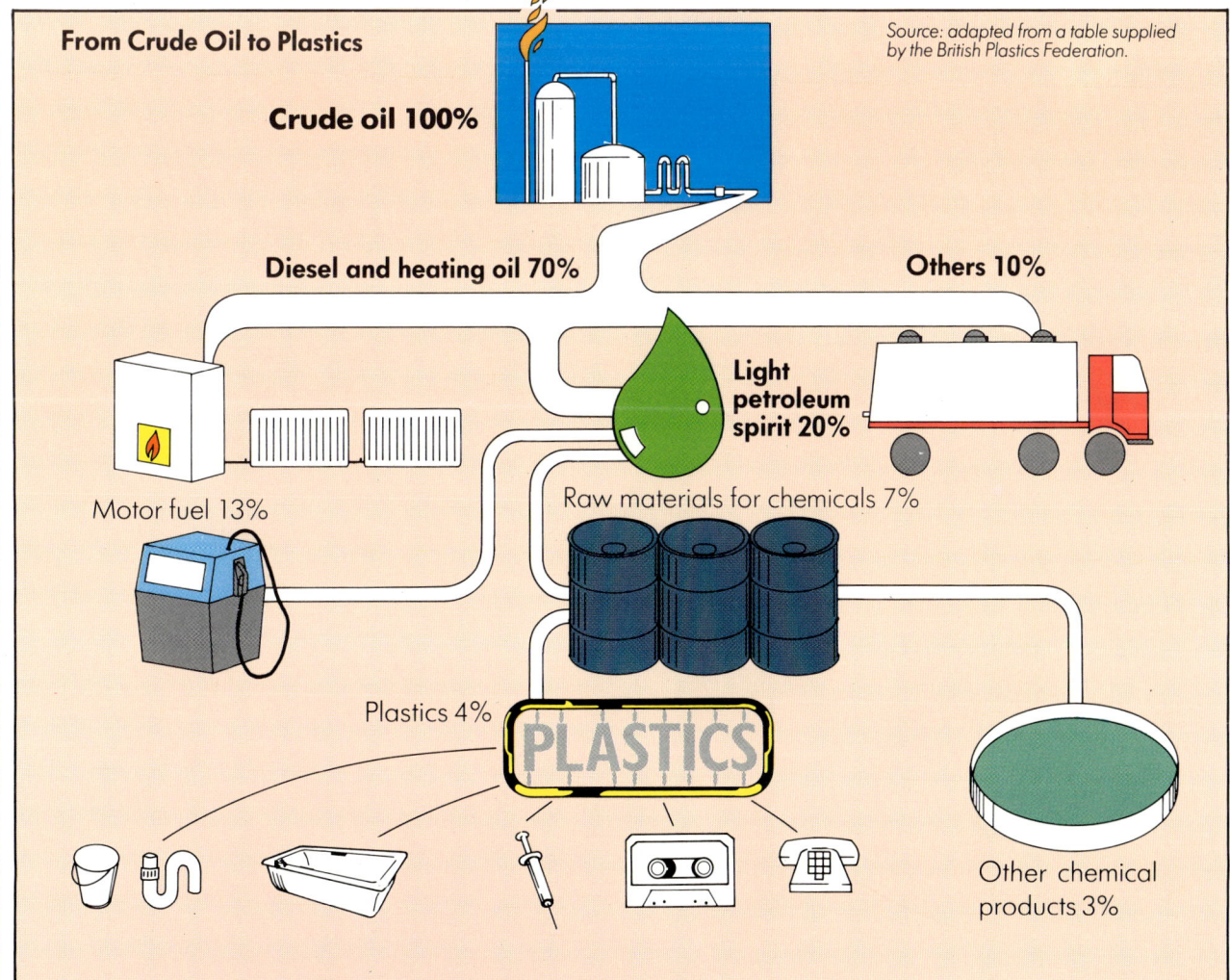

From Crude Oil to Plastics

Source: adapted from a table supplied by the British Plastics Federation.

Crude oil 100%

Diesel and heating oil 70%

Others 10%

Light petroleum spirit 20%

Motor fuel 13%

Raw materials for chemicals 7%

Plastics 4%

PLASTICS

Other chemical products 3%

make them clearer and tougher. PET bottles for fizzy drinks are made in this way. Films too can be stretched (in a different way) and, for example, another plastic, nylon, is used for boil-in-bag foods such as frozen fish (their sharp bones might puncture other films). Stretched PET film is used as roasting bags for cooking chickens at oven temperatures up to 200°C.

More information about processing plastics is available from The British Plastics Federation and its book *The World of Plastics* (see page 47 for details).

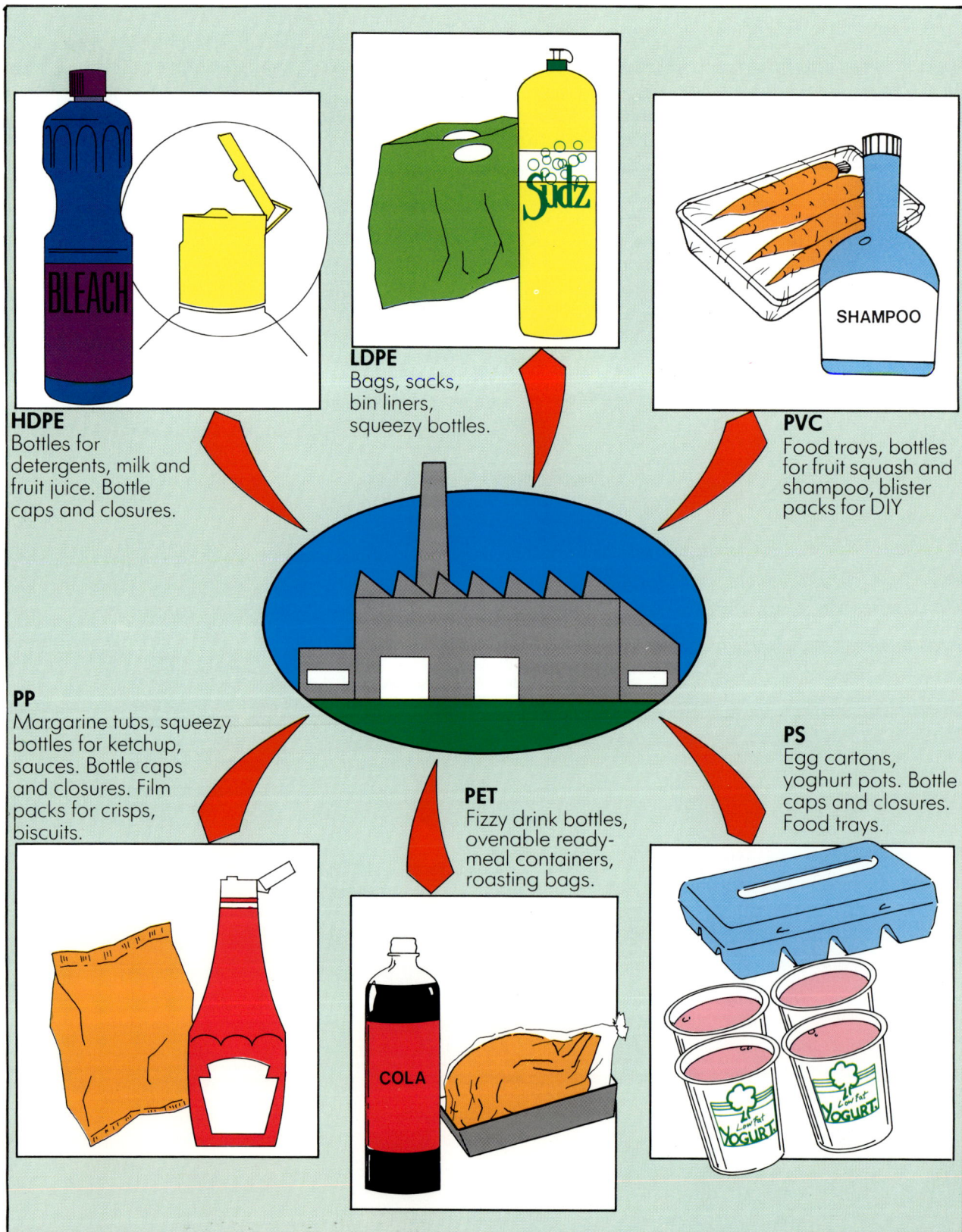

HDPE
Bottles for detergents, milk and fruit juice. Bottle caps and closures.

LDPE
Bags, sacks, bin liners, squeezy bottles.

PVC
Food trays, bottles for fruit squash and shampoo, blister packs for DIY

BLEACH

Sudz

SHAMPOO

PP
Margarine tubs, squeezy bottles for ketchup, sauces. Bottle caps and closures. Film packs for crisps, biscuits.

PET
Fizzy drink bottles, ovenable ready-meal containers, roasting bags.

PS
Egg cartons, yoghurt pots. Bottle caps and closures. Food trays.

COLA

Low Fat YOGURT

Low Fat YOGURT

Matching the product with the packaging

Different products need different protection. Packaging manufacturers have to choose the right material for each product. For example, some foods such as oils, fat and coffee are affected by light and oxygen. Some foods, like biscuits, absorb moisture, others such as meat dry up, and others like milk and mineral water can absorb smells and tastes.

Over 60% of plastics packaging is used for food and drink. From the chart you can see that some similar products are packed in plastics from different families. Each of these families of plastics polymers has its own special properties and they can be as different from each other as metal is from glass. Each family includes many individual types or grades and each grade can be tailored to have a different balance of properties to suit the package needed.

The choice of grade depends on which properties and cost are wanted. For example, stiff and tough PET is needed for large bottles of cola, combining the ability to keep fizz in and smells out. PP cans for emulsion paint are resistant to rust as well as rigid and tough for storage and stacking. A combination of temperature performance and barrier to oxygen and moisture is needed for packaged processed foods like meats, fish and cheese.

The packaging of frozen foods, which are often blast-frozen at −40°C, has to withstand extreme cold, and so LDPE, HDPE and PET are used. For foods that have to be refrigerated or chilled, but not frozen, such as desserts and fresh vegetables, PP, PS and PVC are commonly used.

Polypropylene (PP) can also withstand high temperatures and is used to produce, for example, medical dishes, which have to be sterilised at 120°C.

Plastics can be made into many convenient shapes and sizes and are often used in combination with other materials. Look at the layers in your empty juice or milk cartons and you'll see that plastics films or coatings have been included. Plastics coatings on aluminium foil make it heat sealable (allow it to be sealed without glues) in packets of dried soups and sauces and some chocolate bars. Some coffee packs use laminates of polyester films and aluminium foil. The print is protected by putting it on the underside of the film, so it is sandwiched between the film and the foil. Shrink sleeves on glass bottles help to reduce glass weight and improve safety.

Lighter weight rigid packs and thinner films for flexible packaging have been developed to help keep costs down and to reduce the amount of energy used in each package. At the same time, design and technology is improving the ability of plastics to preserve and protect products, and to add to the convenience of modern lifestyles. In return for these advantages remember to think of other people, to care for the environment and put empty packages in a dustbin or litter bin.

WHAT YOU CAN DO

Look in the fridge and cupboards at home. How many of the products are wrapped or contained in plastic? Write a list of the products you have found and for each one say why you think the manufacturers chose to use plastic.

Paper and board

Paper and board are made from wood pulp (which comes from fibres found in trees) and waste paper. Board is manufactured in the same way as paper but it is thicker and heavier.

Worldwide, of the trees that are cut down each year, nearly three-quarters are removed to clear land for agriculture or used as fuel. The rest are used for commercial logging, producing timber for building, and products like furniture and toys. Paper is generally made from the thinnings, those parts of trees which are too small for use as timber, and the waste from sawmills.

Paper is mainly used for paper bags, labels and as one of the layers in lamination (layers of paper, foil or plastics bound together). Board is used in cartons and drums. Another product is *corrugated board* which is made from layers of paper and used where strong protection is needed such as in packing cases for electrical goods (television, radios, cookers, etc) and for chemicals, books, pharmaceuticals and food packs. Because of the 'fluting' (the wavy layer in some cardboard boxes), it can absorb reasonable impact, making it especially useful for transport by road, air or sea. We recycle a lot of paper and board in this country. Most of it is used to make paper and board for packaging.

Paper and board packaging is useful because

- the materials are light, easy to handle, store, fold and crease;

- if combined with foil or plastic to form laminated packaging, special features are possible such as a seal that prevents evaporation and preserves the product;

- colour printing to a very high quality is possible.

WHAT YOU CAN DO

1 Collect some examples of paper and board packaging:
(a) paper bags
(b) labels
(c) corrugated board
(d) a carton for liquid (fruit juice or milk)
(e) drums which are partly foil or plastics (a custard powder or gravy drum)
(f) cartons such as containers for cereals or frozen foods
(g) boards that can be used in an oven at high temperatures or in a refrigerator at very low temperatures.

2 For each example, explain in your own words:
(a) the special features of this type of packaging
(b) why it is particularly useful for the product
(c) what you like about it.

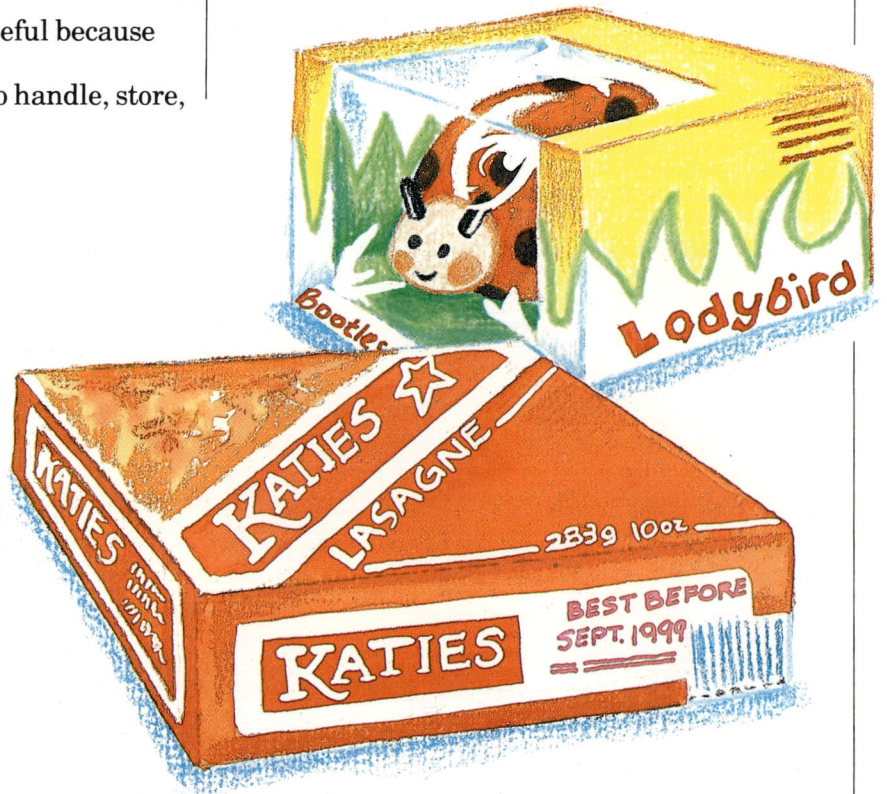

Labels

Labels provide information about a product. They generally describe it – shoes, peas, shoe polish, salt or whatever – unless it is very obvious. For instance, if it's a shirt, the packaging may not say 'shirt'! Secondly, the label gives the maker's name. Thirdly, the law requires information on the contents, weight and the manufacturer or importer. The manufacturer may also have to provide special information, for example, about safety such as for very strong glues, weedkillers and medicines. The label may tell you how to open it, how to use the contents or suggest recipes. If food is likely to be eaten out of doors, the label often carries a 'tidyman' symbol. The packaging may also have details of a special offer or a competition. Finally, there may also be a bar code on the label. This is used by shops and supermarkets that have a computerised checkout system to help them keep a close control on stock, and also to save time at the checkouts.

Labels are usually helpful but sometimes the instructions can be misleading. For example, once upon a time a stick deodorant carried a label which said 'twist and push up bottom'. It didn't carry that label for very long!

WHAT YOU CAN DO

1 Look at the labels from a new plastic Heinz tomato sauce bottle. Make a list of:
(a) the manufacturer's name and address
(b) the name of the product
(c) the weight of the contents
(d) special instructions to be noted by the customer
how the bottle is sealed
nutritional information, explaining what the product is made from (its ingredients)
any special offers available to customers
anything new about the design of this container.

Is there a bar code on the label?

2 Collect some labels that attract you particularly and say why you like them.

3 Choose one of the products below and design your own label for it. You must add all the information that is essential. Choose from:
(a) a hair mousse
(b) a label for a new 'delicious, crunchy, tasty biscuit'
(c) a soft drink bottle or can
(d) a can of peaches in their own juice.

Your design should illustrate that you have thought about and solved problems of:
- *graphics* (pictures and text)
- *promotion* (selling the product to the consumer).

HEINZ TOMATO KETCHUP
NEW SQUEEZABLE!
5142/F ℮ 460 g

HEINZ TOMATO KETCHUP
5142/H
Heinz Ketchup is made from pure natural ingredients entirely free from artificial colours, flavours or thickeners.
In fact, the red colour comes only from juicy red ripe tomatoes. There are no artificial preservatives added to Heinz Tomato Ketchup. We prefer to rely on the traditional ingredients – sugar, vinegar, salt – as natural preservatives.

NUTRITION INFORMATION

Typical Values	Amount per 100g	Amount per level dessert spoon (10ml)
Fat	trace	trace
(of which saturates)	(Nil)	(Nil)
Protein	1.0g	0.1g
Carbohydrate	24.9g	2.8g
(of which sugars)	(24.9g)	(2.8g)
Energy	415 kJ/ 97 kcal	47 kJ/ 11 kcal
Sodium	1.1g	0.1g
Dietary Fibre	1.3g	0.1g

INGREDIENTS: TOMATOES, SUGAR, SPIRIT VINEGAR, SALT, SPICES

5015 7556

BEST BEFORE END – SEE CAP
5142/J
Heinz
MADE IN ENGLAND
H.J.HEINZ CO.LTD.
HAYES, MIDDX. UB4 8AL

NEW SQUEEZABLE! BOTTLE

UNSCREW CAP AND REMOVE FOIL SEAL BEFORE USE
SHAKE BEFORE USING
REFRIGERATE AFTER OPENING

Making cartons

Who invented the first carton?

The story starts over a hundred years ago, in New York, USA. A printer, Robert Gair, who made paper bags, produced a carton from strong paper and board.

By accident rather than intention he discovered a method of creasing and cutting cartonboard in one operation and thus invented the folding carton.

The process was adopted by the Kellogg Corporation for their range of breakfast cereals and other foods, and the carton had arrived to stay.

Today, the manufacture of cartons is a massive business: in the UK alone over 500,000 tonnes of board are used every year to produce cartons worth over £600 million. That's some business!

But what *is* a carton? It is a container made from cartonboard whose thickness is 250 microns or more. Its shape can be square, rectangular, triangular or octagonal. It can be glued, stitched, folded, tacked or locked and can be printed on.

To make cartons, sheets of board are printed and then stamped out to the required shape and size. At the same time, another stamp puts creases where the board is to be folded. The flat cartons can then be sent direct to the manufacturer who makes the carton up, fills it with the product and then glues and folds the ends. If the manufacturer wants the carton to be pre-glued, the carton maker can add a line of glue to one edge.

Some cartons have very special qualities. For example, look at the packs for fish fingers. You'll see the pack is made from plastic coated boards. The carton is formed and sealed by using a hot air blast, instead of using glue. Why do you think that glue isn't used for fish fingers and other food products?

Coatings are added to cartons to give extra protection. A layer of polythene is added: this protects the food contents from contamination by air or moisture. For an even longer life, a layer of aluminium is added.

Metals

Tinplate and aluminium are used a great deal in packaging, to produce cans, aerosols, foil containers and metal closures. There are various ways to make cans. Some cans are made of three pieces of metal (tinplate) – most food cans are of this type. Other cans are made from two pieces of metal (either aluminium or tinplate) and are used mainly for pet foods and drinks. About half of these drinks cans are made from aluminium, the others are tinplate.

More than 10,000 million food, pet food and drinks cans are bought every year, with most homes using about ten cans every week.

Can you think of some of the advantages of canning food?

1 Canned food keeps well. As long as the cans are kept in a cool, dry cupboard, the food can last for months or years.

2 They are very convenient because the food has already been cooked and can be eaten straight from the can or re-heated.

3 There is no need to add preservatives to canned food because the preserving is carried out in the cooking and canning process.

4 No food is wasted. (Well, do you leave any beans or peaches at the bottom of the tin?)

5 Drinks cans are a convenient size, can be easily opened, are lightweight and are easy to chill.

The food canning process

The stages in canning are:

1 The food is prepared for canning.

2 The cans are cleaned by powerful jet blowers and rinsed in purified water.

3 As the open cans move along a conveyor belt, the food is put into them, and a liquid (brine for vegetables, syrup or fruit juice for fruit) is added.

4 They are then moved on to a can-closing machine, and sealed. Each can is checked to make sure it has the right content level: any shortfilled cans are automatically rejected.

5 The cans are placed into a machine rather like a giant pressure cooker. The food is cooked and sterilised, and the cans are cooled.

6 The conveyor moves on again. At this stage the cans are usually packed in 24s and the outer packaging is put on. They are placed by machine on to cardboard trays, glued into place and the whole pack is then shrink-wrapped in film and heat-sealed. Some cans are packed in cases made from board.

7 The final stage comes when the trays are loaded onto pallets and taken to a warehouse. Lorries collect them and take them to shops and supermarkets throughout the country.

The making of a 2-piece drinks can

1 Coil Coils of aluminium or tin-plate provide the raw material for cans.

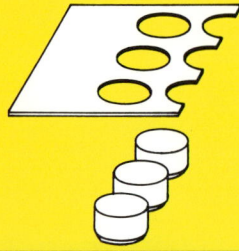

2 Cupping press Stamps discs and forms cups from the coil.

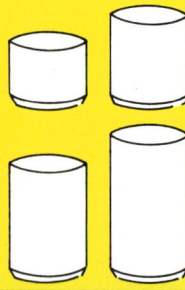

3 Wall ironers The wall ironers are the heart of the Drawn and Ironed process, converting the cups into untrimmed cans.

4 Trimmer Trimmers remove the irregular edge of the cans, trimming them to a precise height.

5 Washing In the washer the cans are cleaned and dried in preparation for internal and external coatings.

6 Coater A coater provides the outside wall of the can with a protective coating and base colour.

7 Oven Coated cans are dried in a gas-fired hot air oven.

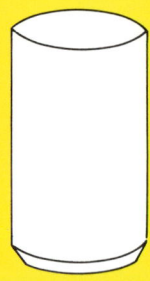

8 Decorator The decorator applies the the design to the can in up to six colours.

9 Rim coater A coat of varnish is applied to the base by the bottom rim coater.

10 Internal lacquer Spray machines apply an internal coating or protective lacquer to maintain product quality.

11 Internal curing The internal coating of the can is dried in the final bake oven.

12 Necker Flanger The necker flanger shapes the can so that the end will fit onto it.

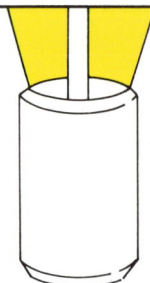

13 Tester Cans are tested at all stages of manufacture and finally 100% checked in a high-speed tester.

14 Palletising and warehousing Cans pass to the warehouse for palletising and despatch.

15 Despatch Cans and ends delivered to customer.

16 Filling Cans are filled on high-speed lines and the ends seamed on.

Source: The Can Makers' Association

Aerosols

How many aerosols do you think your family use in a year? The average is about 20. Forty years ago there weren't any aerosols – why do we need them today?

Aerosols protect and contain a product just like any other form of packaging. They are popular because they dispense as well as store material. For example, you can spray deodorants, air fresheners, polish or paint from the same container that they're kept in. Aerosol paints have another special quality – they produce a fine finish that couldn't be matched by a brush. Expensive perfume is best kept in an aerosol because air can't get to it, and only a little of the perfume is used at a time. Most aerosols are made from metal, but a few are made of glass or plastic with a cap or valve. They work by mixing the product (paint, perfume or a drug) with a solvent (which is also a propellant) which forces the product through the valve.

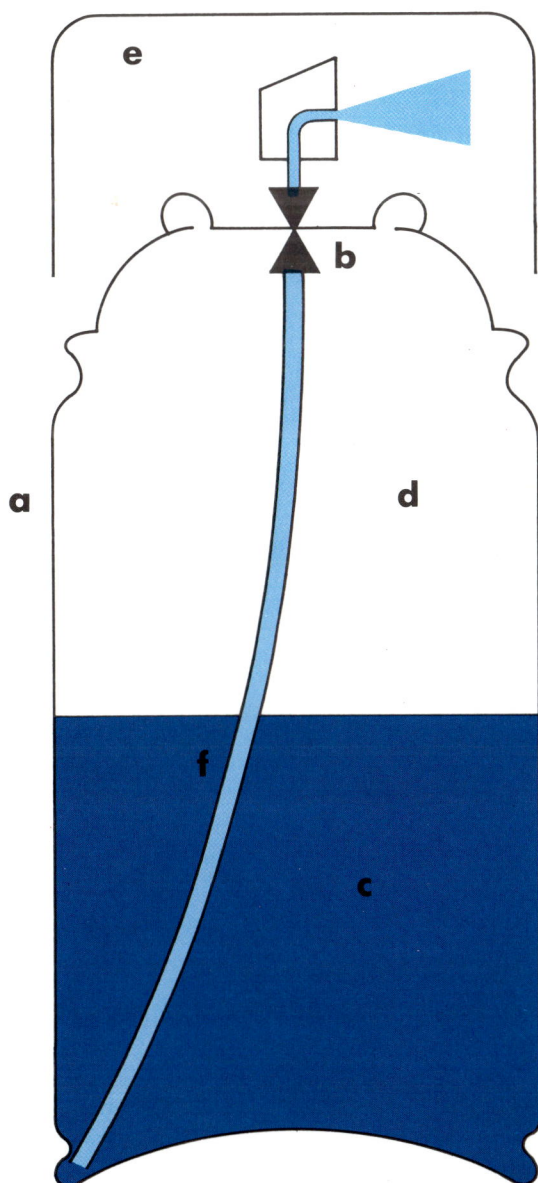

Yet, despite their usefulness, aerosols are not popular with some people. Do you know why?

1 One view is that they might explode on a plane. Untrue.

2 Paint aerosols are used by vandals for graffiti. True.

3 Some aerosols contain gases called CFCs which may damage the ozone layer. True.

CFCs were first used in refrigerators and air conditioning and this is still a big use. They are also used to produce some expanded plastics. It is possible that CFCs react with the ozone layer in the stratosphere (upper atmosphere). This layer protects the earth from harmful radiation from the sun. If the ozone layer is damaged, it could increase the risk of some kinds of skin cancer. Some aerosols, however, for pharmaceutical products, have to use CFCs because alternatives are not suitable.

In 1987 a number of countries, including the UK, agreed to limit the use of CFCs and scientists are trying to find other things that will do the same jobs. Already, in the UK, 30% of aerosols do not contain CFCs and this trend is likely to continue rapidly. Other kinds of propellants already in use include nitrous oxide (laughing gas) which has always been used in aerosols for cream.

What do you think?

1 Find out more about aerosols (BAMA will help – the address is at the back of this book). Write out the reasons *for* using aerosols as packaging, and then write out the reasons *against* using them.

2 In your student group, discuss your opinions and findings. What does the group think about the use of aerosols – for and against?

How aerosols work

The diagram shows the main parts of an aerosol:

(a) The container, usually made of tinplate or aluminium.

(b) A valve, incorporating a button (or actuator).

(c) The product and liquefied gas.

(d) Stored energy.

(e) An overcap.

(f) Diptube.

Glass

Glass is one of the oldest of the packaging materials. So old, that collectors go around antique shops, searching for old beer – and other – bottles. Today, glass making is a huge business and glass is a very popular choice for some foods.

The advantages of glass are:

- you can see the contents clearly

- glass bottles and jars can be opened and resealed easily

- glass does not affect the taste of the food inside

- glass is impermeable which means that liquids and gases cannot leak into or out of it

- some glass containers can be washed and re-used

- the raw materials used to make glass (sand, limestone, soda ash) are cheap and in plentiful supply

- used bottles and jars can be saved in 'bottle banks' and recycled in a furnace to make more glass.

Can you think of any other advantages? What about the disadvantages? Can you think of any?

One of the problems with glass is its heaviness compared with other materials. Another is that glass can break.

WHAT YOU CAN DO

1 In your notebook, summarise in your own words the advantages, and the disadvantages of using glass in packaging.

2 Write out a list of goods that are packaged in glass. How many of them are jars (with wide necks) and how many are bottles (with narrow necks)? What do they contain? Explain why glass is particularly useful and attractive to the manufacturers of these products.

3 Glass is now less popular than some other forms of packaging. Why do you think this is?

Caps and closures

Caps and closures are words used by the packaging industry to describe anything that closes or seals a container. A 'cap' usually means a screw-threaded closure that fits over the neck of a container and which can be used to reseal it. A 'closure' is any other kind of seal. They have the same purposes – to stop the contents from escaping and to prevent anything else from getting in.

Closures are made from metal and plastics. They vary from simple foil caps used for milk bottles to precisely manufactured caps, for products such as baby foods.

WHAT YOU CAN DO

1 What products are shown in these pictures? Draw and describe the different types of closure that you can see here.

2 Collect a dozen or more different caps and closures from medicine bottles, fruit jars, drinks and detergent bottles, tubes and boxes. Write down the special features of each one – how it works, what it's made of, its design and anything which has been printed on it.

Snack packaging – CASE STUDY

'Crisp and tasty'

Most people take it for granted that the crispy snacks they buy will be crisp and tasty. But for the manufacturer this is a big challenge. In the factory, straight out of the oven, potato crisps are in perfect condition but how can the manufacturer make sure they stay this way on the journey from the factory to the shops and then to the home? It might be days or even weeks before they are eaten.

Packaging can help. But what does it have to do?

- Moisture in the outside air must be kept out.
- Flavour must be kept in and smells kept out.
- Strong light can make fried foods go rancid, so must be kept out.
- The snacks need to keep their nutritional value.
- A pack that does the job in a temperate climate like the UK might not be good enough in a tropical climate.

Some people now want to have the choice when buying a snack as to which additives are included. If some additives are removed, then the food may need more protection by improving the barrier properties of the pack. So, when designing a snack pack, there are many points to consider including:

- the type of food; how long it will keep fresh
- selecting the right plastic film to give the right protection
- economics: how much does the packaging cost?
- air tight seals (even the best possible pack is no good if it comes undone).

This ICI case study looks mainly at one aspect of all these problems – the effects of moisture on different packs and sizes of packs for potato crisps. No one wants crisps without the crunch,

and you might be surprised to learn that the size of pack actually can affect how crunchy crisps are!

Research

ICI's team analysed packs from different countries. In many European countries, people like small packs of between 20 and 30 grammes, whereas in the USA people prefer 'giant' packs 10 times the size and even larger. The researchers first wanted to find out how much packaging film was needed to wrap up crisps in different size packs. The way they did this is shown in figure 1. On the horizontal axis the weight of the food in the pack is shown and the vertical axis shows the amount of film used per unit of food weight. You can see that the ratios for heavier packs are smaller than those for lighter packs; in other words the bigger the pack the smaller the amount of film needed per crisp.

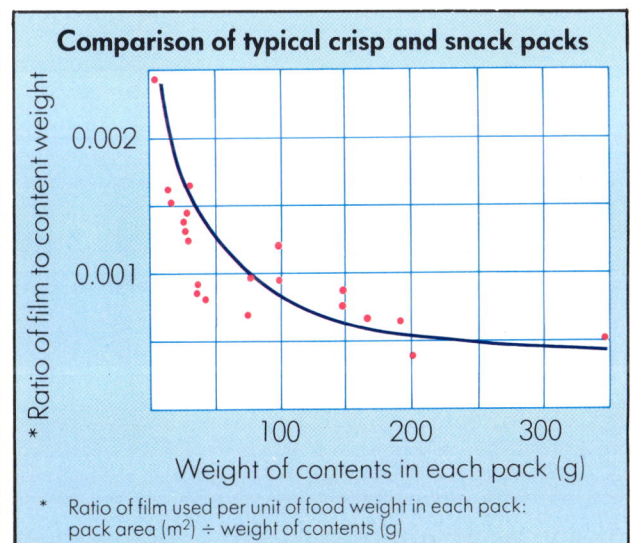

Comparison of typical crisp and snack packs

Vertical axis: * Ratio of film to content weight (0.002, 0.001)
Horizontal axis: Weight of contents in each pack (g) (100, 200, 300)

* Ratio of film used per unit of food weight in each pack: pack area (m²) ÷ weight of contents (g)

Figure 1

One of the family of plastics, oriented polypropylene film (OPP), is often used for crisp packs. Tests on 14 different types of OPP film and different sizes of pack, (using 'Propafilm', the ICI trade name for OPP film), were carried out in laboratory and real-life conditions.

Three types of conditions were used:

Condition 1 a laboratory with controlled temperature like a warm summer's day with quite dry atmosphere
Condition 2 a temperate chamber which has a temperature and humidity like a hot summer's day after a rainy spell
Condition 3 a tropical chamber – very hot and wet like the tropical house at Kew Gardens.

Comparison of moisture increase with pack size and film type

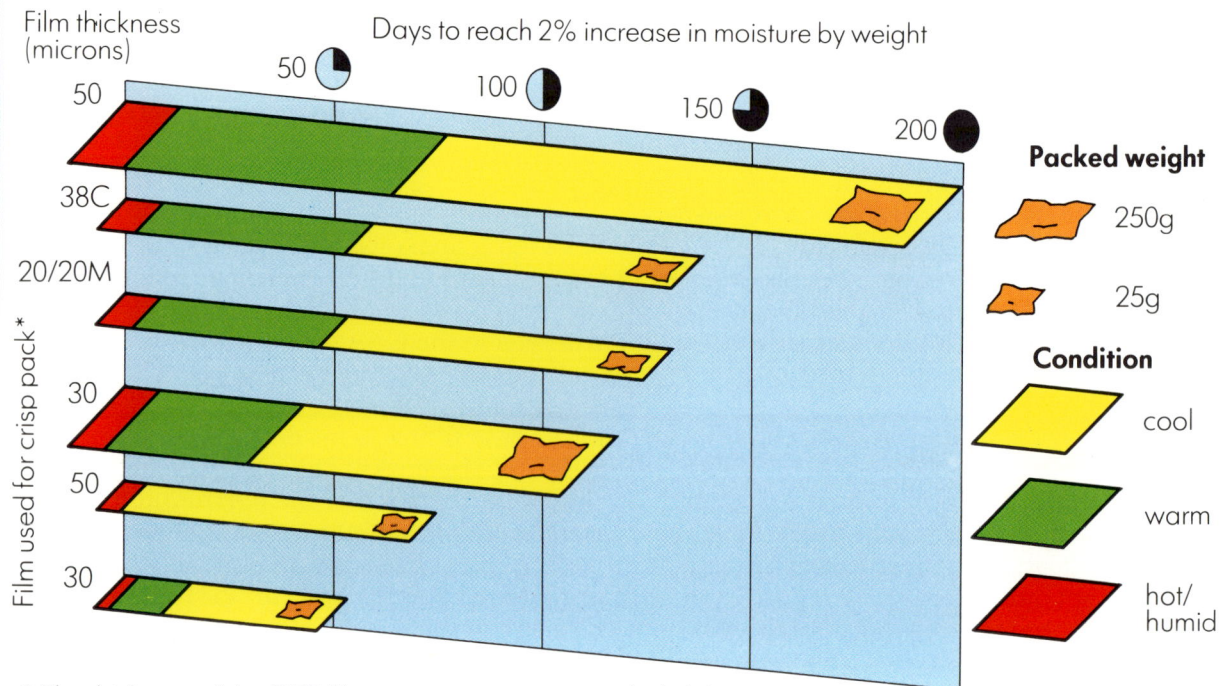

Film thickness (microns)

Days to reach 2% increase in moisture by weight

50 | 100 | 150 | 200

Film used for crisp pack*

38C
20/20M
30
50
30

Packed weight
250g
25g

Condition
cool
warm
hot/humid

* The thickness of the OPP films is given in microns in the left-hand column. 38C is a barrier coated OPP film. 20/20 M is a laminate of OPP and barrier metallised OPP film. The other 4 are plain OPP films.

Figure 2

The amount of moisture taken up by the crisps was worked out by measuring the gain in weight of the contents in each individual pack, and showing the time taken to reach a 2% increase. The figure of 2% gain was used to measure each crisp pack because the people on the test panel judged this to be still an acceptable level of crispness.

ICI's research results with some of the films are shown in figure 2 above.

The best protection against moisture was given by the biggest packs kept in the controlled laboratory conditions. But manufacturers can't expect us all to want to buy huge packs or to live in a laboratory.

WHAT YOU CAN DO

1 What is your favourite crisp? What would you like to test it for? Work out a test that you could carry out on a packet of crisps.

2 What comparisons can you make from the bar chart? What types of film helped to delay the moisture uptake of small packs?

3 What other ways can you think of to improve the packaging of crisps?

Consultation

The manufacturer starts by talking to people who are going to be involved. A key person is the supplier of the printed film (the film converter). He also needs to ask the people who will handle, sell and finally eat the crisps what they want – and that includes YOU because, however good the pack and the food might seem to the converter and manufacturer, if you – the customer – don't like it, you won't buy it and the others are all out of business.

There are other people whose views count too, such as producers of packaging machinery. Of course, someone has to get the crisps to the shops and they have to be fitted into a lorry in reasonable quantities. This is the job of the distributor. Someone else has to sell the crisps – the shopkeeper or retailer. He wants something that he can stack on the shelves and that lasts long enough for customers to buy before the 'sell by' date.

So, next time you munch through a packet of crisps, stop and think of all the work that went into getting them to you. And don't stop there. When you've eaten all the crisps, remember to think of other people, care for the environment and put the empty packet in a dustbin or litter bin.

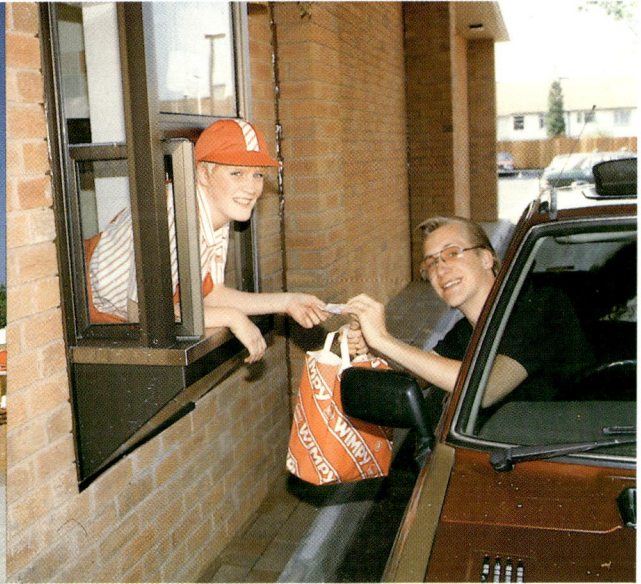

Recently, a new packaging challenge has been introduced to Wimpy restaurants. One of the latest developments is a 'drive-in' restaurant. Customers don't need to leave their cars to be served. They can choose to order and collect the food without leaving their car and then eat in the car or at home. Think of the problems – and the opportunities – that this development presented for Wimpy. Among the features that had to be considered were:

● The customers in their cars didn't have knives and forks, plates and washing up bowls. How is this to be tackled?

● How would the cooked food be packaged so that it kept hot and didn't spoil customers' clothes?

● How would the packaging be disposed of?

WHAT YOU CAN DO

1 Wimpy have solved these problems: drive-in restaurants have been opened in several parts of the UK. But suppose you were presented with these packaging problems. What solutions would you suggest? Explain (with drawings, perhaps) what kind of packaging you would use for a drive-in restaurant.

2 Next time you visit a counter-service Wimpy restaurant, carry out a survey of the different kinds of packaging you see there. Collect samples of the packaging and explain why you think they were chosen.

Toys need a special kind of packaging. Why? Because toys are in a very competitive market. Toy-makers in the UK and overseas have to compete with each other in 'customer-appeal', price and value-for-money.

Corgi Toys Ltd makes toys of all kinds but most of its business is in 'die-cast' toys such as cars. Market research showed that Corgi needed a new 'image' (abandoning its dog symbol) and new packaging. This is an example, therefore, of packaging being used for advertising, marketing and customer-appeal, as well as for protection and containment.

As you can see from the illustration on the right, the first thing to change was the symbol. Instead of a dog, a car was shown coming out of the name Corgi. This gives the impression of speed (a car racing along the road) and fun.

The new packaging used strong, bright colours (red, blue, yellow, green, black) to give impact. There were traffic signs on the pack to show 'street life', a theme that runs through all the designs. Not many words were used: pictures tell the story, as you can see. And the pack has a film window so that you can see the product quite clearly.

WHAT YOU CAN DO

1 In your group, discuss the new packaging design. Do you think it works? Can you say why, or why not?

2 You can work on this task alone or in groups of 2, 3 or 4 students. You are a toy manufacturer which makes a toy zoo, a 'take-apart' racing car and a chatter telephone, as shown in the drawings. Suggest methods of packaging for one of them. Illustrate your answer with drawings and explanations such as the kind of packaging you would recommend and any special problems or possibilities that you can think of.

New products are essential to any business. For a food manufacturing company, this means developing new products and using packaging which attracts new customers, eager to buy, eat and enjoy them. It was this kind of thinking that led to pizza pies, Yorkie bars, muesli bars, Penguin biscuits and many other well-known products.

A new idea please ...

A team of four young people who work for a food company have been given the daunting task of suggesting, making and designing a new packet of biscuits.

The team is:

1 Alison is a marketing manager: she's had lots of experience in marketing biscuits.

2 Sharon is a designer who specialises in food packaging design.

3 Andrew is a plant manager at one of the company's factories. He's going to have to organise the mass production of the biscuits.

4 The fourth member of the team is ... YOU. You have been called in to give additional advice.
So let's get going ...

Planning

Alison began by working out what customers would be looking for in a new biscuit and what would make it successful from the company's viewpoint. She made a list of the important factors to be borne in mind when planning the new biscuit. This is where she asked for your advice. Look at the factors listed below. Rank them 1 to 13 from the most to the least important.

1 A new taste
2 Healthy eating
 (ie using wholemeal flour)
3 The biscuit looks appetising
4 Attractive packaging
5 It looks like a home-baked biscuit
6 Launch date
7 Trial marketing
8 Cost of production
9 The selling price is right: value for money for the customer and profitable for the company
10 Plant (factory lines) availability
11 It can be eaten between meals or as a snack
12 It doesn't compete with other biscuits sold by your company
13 Shelf-life (how long it will keep fresh unopened)

Market research – what does the customer want?

Next, the team asked potential customers for their opinions. People in shops, stores, on the street, at home and at work were asked what they'd like in a new biscuit. Lots of ideas were put forward but most people voted for a rich, rough-textured crunchy biscuit that 'melted in the mouth'.

Bake and taste

Alison's next job was to ask the home economics staff to come up with a recipe. After many recipes, alternative ingredients and lots of experimental cooking, the home economics people suggested a special recipe which they thought people would like.

Their recipe was for an oatmeal and wholemeal flour biscuit (good for healthy eating) that looked brown, crispy and appetising. Here's a picture of the biscuits.

'Let's try them' said Alison. The company team liked them. Customers who were given samples said they liked the new product. So the team decided to risk going to the next stage.

Production

Now Andrew's work started. His job was to organise the baking, production and wrapping of the biscuits in tens of thousands.

Packaging

How would they be packaged? This problem wasn't left until last. Sharon had been at work on it for months. But now she needs help and again the team calls for your assistance.

From what you have learned in this book, which of these alternatives would you recommend:

● In a box, designed as a gift?

● In tens or dozens, film-wrapped?

● Individually wrapped in a packet?

● In a paper bag, sealed and film-wrapped?

● Any other method – you suggest it.

To help you, here are some of the same company's biscuits in their own special wrapping.

Give them a name

And, finally, the name. Lots of people have been thinking about it – Alison, Sharon, the marketing staff and the company's directors. But no one has come up with the ideal name. Again, they call for your expertise. What do you suggest as a name for this new biscuit? Design, draw and describe the pack that you'd suggest, with its name clearly shown on the labelled packaging.

Packaging innovation and development has been an important feature in the success of the world's most famous soft drink – Coca-Cola. Sold in 155 countries throughout the world, the Coca-Cola trade mark is seen on a wide variety of packages.

The story began in a backyard in Atlanta, Georgia, USA in 1886, when pharmacist John Pemberton produced the first Coca-Cola syrup, which was sold in Jacob's Pharmacy in Atlanta for 5 cents a glass. In its early days, Coca-Cola syrup was mixed with water and sold by the glass in American 'soda fountains' or cafes. This method of serving Coca-Cola imposed severe limits on providing the product outside Atlanta; the key to increasing the sales of Coca-Cola lay in widening its distribution.

In 1890, a businessman from Tennessee obtained exclusive rights to bottle the soda fountain product and to distribute Coca-Cola throughout the USA. Almost overnight, Coca-Cola became available in bottles, in a much wider variety of outlets all over the USA. Sales were no longer restricted to outlets which had installed the soda fountain equipment. Simply by placing the finished product into a package, the company could contain and preserve the drink for a long period of time.

The Coca-Cola Company realised very early that it needed to help customers recognise the difference between their original product, and

other copy products seeking to share in its success. In 1915 the famous fluted contour bottle was designed; by 1916 the bottle was used throughout the USA and it is still in use today all over the world.

As consumer demand for Coca-Cola grew, the company and its bottlers recognised the need to develop new packages. In 1922 initial research began into the six-pack – six bottles packed in a cardboard carton, providing the consumer with a convenient carry-home pack, which also served as a handy means of collecting and returning the empty bottles for re-filling.

Until 1955 the 6.5oz glass contour bottle remained the primary package for Coca-Cola. By then, however, it was obvious that there was a demand for other forms of packaging which were better suited to rapidly changing lifestyles. The Coca-Cola Company began to develop new formats and new sizes to provide consumers with the most convenient packaging, some returnable and some non-returnable. In 1960, for example, 12oz (now the 330ml) flat-topped cans were

introduced and later the Company introduced ring pulls to provide easy opening. Today, Coca-Cola and Schweppes Beverages Limited, who provide Coca-Cola products in Great Britain, operate the most modern soft drink canning line in the world filling 2,000 cans per minute.

Consumer demand called for Coca-Cola in larger bottles for consumption at home. Originally these were of glass – they often still are – but in 1978 the polyethylene terephthalate bottle, or PET as it is known, was introduced as a lightweight plastic package for larger volume sales. PET bottles now appear in various sizes including 1.5 litre, 2 litre and 3 litre.

The idea of multipackaging is widely used. In 1987 the six-pack was introduced for purchase in supermarkets. Consumers can buy six cans

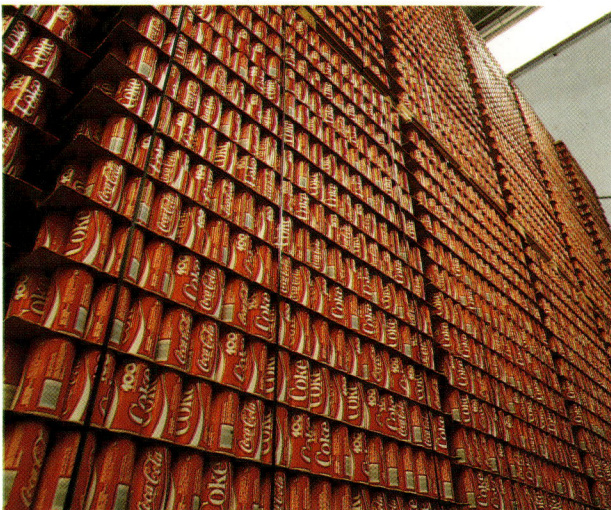

packaged by a plastic device known as Hi-Cone, which holds them together. The PET bottle and the six-pack are just two examples of the types of packaging used for Coca-Cola. And The Coca-Cola Company continues to develop new packaging ideas. In 1985 a special can was developed for use in space, helping the astronauts to enjoy one of their favourite drinks at zero gravity!

Remember, as much as you enjoy drinking Coca-Cola, you should always dispose of these cans properly.

WHAT YOU CAN DO

1 The Coca-Cola trade mark now appears on several products including diet Coca-Cola and cherry Coca-Cola. Collect as many different examples as you can of these products and write a line or two about each of them, and how they are packaged.

2 Suppose Coca-Cola wanted a new slogan to be just as successful as 'Delicious and Refreshing'. What slogan would you suggest? Design and draw your own idea as an advert for Coca-Cola using the famous name, your slogan and an appropriate picture or drawing – perhaps a sporting personality, or an illustration of eating and drinking or an idea of your own.

Many people are rightly concerned that we are using up natural resources such as raw materials and energy. Some people criticise the packaging industry because they think materials such as paper, metal, plastics and glass are wasted on packaging which ends up in the dustbin.

The packaging industry is also concerned about unnecessary waste and is constantly developing ways to avoid it. For example, over the years, packaging for general food and drink products has been made thinner and lighter in weight, so that less material is thrown away when the packaging is no longer needed.

WHAT YOU CAN DO

Look at the statements below and say whether you think they are true or false.

1 Packaging prevents waste by preserving food and stopping it going rotten.

2 By protecting products from being damaged or spoiled, packaging reduces wasted products.

3 Packaging is used as a marketing tool as well as protection.

4 A third of the weight of waste in our dustbins is packaging.

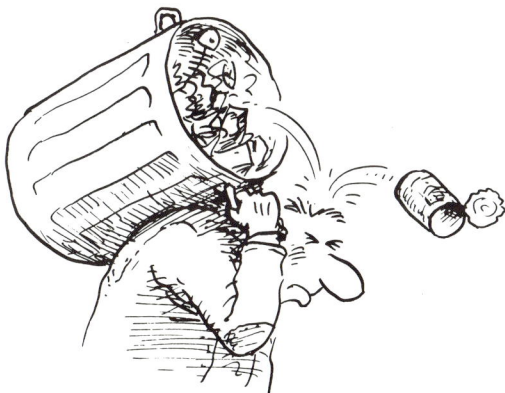

5 In the future, waste disposal costs are likely to rise.

Uses for process waste

Much of our food is prepared and processed centrally and then distributed, protected by packaging. The waste from the product stays at the factory where it can often be used to make other products. For example, in a chicken processing factory, the feathers are taken away first and cleaned and treated for use in duvets and pillows. Other inedible bits – head, feet, and viscera – are used in other products such as gelatine.

Another example is fresh orange juice which is becoming more and more popular as a drink. If we squeezed all the oranges that are needed for the amount we drink today, all the skins would go into the dustbin. As it is, most people buy

orange juice packed in cartons or bottles that has been prepared in a factory. Outside the factory, there are enough orange skins to be worth using for something else. In the USA they are washed and used for other drinks. In Israel they are chopped up and made into a concentrate for squash. In Brazil they are dried out and used as cattle feed.

It's all rubbish

Household waste accounts for about 4% of all waste in this country. What do you think makes up the other 96% of waste? This chart helps you to think of the answer.

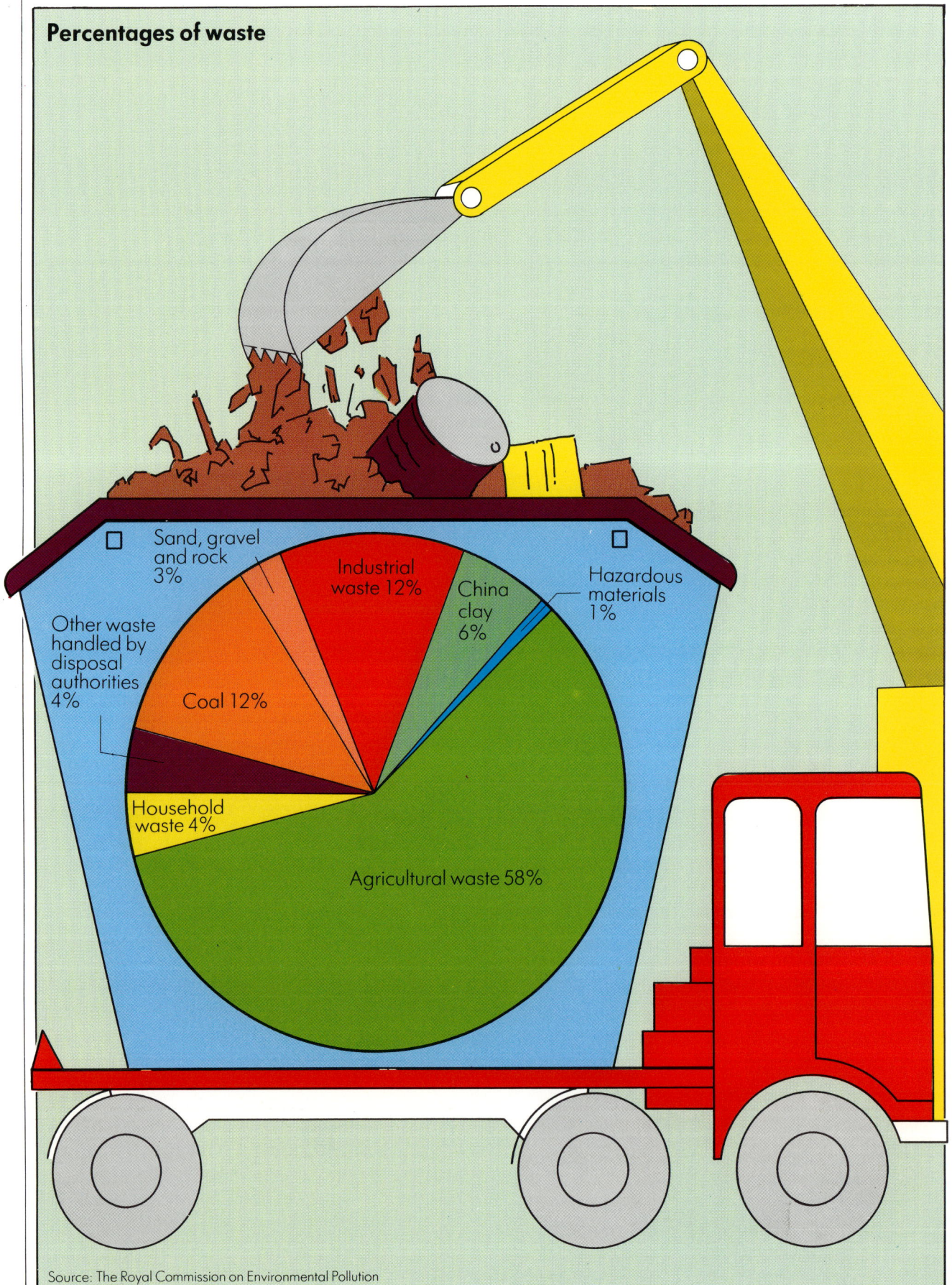

Percentages of waste

Sand, gravel and rock 3%

Industrial waste 12%

China clay 6%

Hazardous materials 1%

Other waste handled by disposal authorities 4%

Coal 12%

Household waste 4%

Agricultural waste 58%

Source: The Royal Commission on Environmental Pollution

36

Where does the waste go?

The dustbin outside your house is probably emptied once a week by the dustman. Have you ever wondered where it goes?

Nearly all of it is put in holes in the ground. This is called land-filling. In this country we dig up lots of minerals, leaving holes. Some are allowed to fill with water and are used as leisure and sports facilities; others are filled in again with rubbish and turned into golf courses, or are sometimes used for agriculture.

The rest of our waste (10%) is burned (incinerated). In some cases the heat made from burning it is used to heat nearby factories or is even turned into electricity.

In future, more rubbish is likely to be burned because there are fewer suitable holes for land-filling near cities and it is expense to transport the waste long distances.

Have you ever felt guilty about throwing something away, not because it was worn out but because you are fed up with it? A pile of old magazines might not interest you any more, but someone else might like to have them. Many items of packaging are also useful to play-groups. For example, plastics bottles can be turned into model spacecraft. Can you think of other uses of waste material?

If you look in the telephone directory 'Yellow Pages' you'll probably find local charities or play groups who could make good use of things you don't want. You can find the address of the National Play Resources Unit at the back of this book.

Recycling

You don't always have to repair something to be able to use it again. Sometimes it is beyond repair but the materials it is made from could be useful to someone; it might be possible to recycle or re-use them. Most of the waste that is recycled comes from industry – very little household waste is recycled. Can you think why?

The recycling of materials is a complicated process. First, the materials have to be collected together. When there are enough to make up a lorry-load, they have to be transported to a plant for cleaning and processing. Some materials are collected by the local authority. The most important point is to make sure that someone can use the materials and that all the transporting and processing does not use up more resources than the materials have in them. For instance, plastics are made from oil. If the lorry that collects the waste plastics and the factory that reprocesses it use more oil than you can get back from the bottle, recycling it is a waste of everybody's time and energy. There are a lot of people working on the design of recycling systems that really save resources but every recycling idea needs to be checked out first.

Tinplate (or steel-based) cans are attracted by a magnet and can be removed from mixed waste. In a few areas, paper is collected separately from other wastes. Other materials such as glass and aluminium need to be collected in a different way and you can help. Lots of towns now have Bottle Banks where you can take glass bottles and jars. Don't throw them in the dustbin but bank them so they can be used to make new glass.

In some areas, other materials are also collected in 'banks'. Find out what happens where you live and how you can help support these schemes.

Some of the things that go into our dustbins have a lot of potential heat energy in them. We say they have a high calorific value; things like old shoes, plastics bottles, fish finger packets. If more of our waste was burned, then even old socks could be useful.

WHAT YOU CAN DO

Choose an item of packaging from home and using pictures/ diagrams show how it could be re-used for another purpose.

For further information on packaging and the environment, write to the Industry Council for Packaging and the Environment (INCPEN). Their address is on page 47.

Litter louts

It's a sad fact that some of the packaging for food and drinks becomes litter. Carelessly thrown away, it spoils the countryside, the streets, parks and open spaces.

Some people blame the food manufacturers and packagers.

'It seems to me that most packaging is simply to get people to buy. If sweets and crisps were not wrapped and packaged, I wouldn't have anything to throw on the ground. And the packaging adds to the price, too!'

Others blame the local authority.

'If there were more litter bins and they weren't always full, I wouldn't drop my rubbish on the ground.'

Other people blame the public – you and me, that is.

'It's disgusting the way that people throw away soft drink cans, old train tickets and apple cores. I've seen it happen hundreds of times. But take-aways are the worst. Next time you're in town, look at the area around a fish shop or the take-away. You'll see greasy trays and boxes. People should be fined.'

WHAT YOU CAN DO

1 In class or in small groups, talk about the *causes* of litter. Is it because of people's thoughtlessness? Or is it the fault of the town and city councils for not putting up more litterbins and emptying full ones? What do you think?

2 What policy does your own local authority (the town or city council) have towards litter? Find out about it and write a short report on what's being done in your area.

3 Design, draw and illustrate a poster which asks people to be more responsible towards litter.

4 Think about what sort of things are thrown away – rail tickets, yesterday's newspapers, drinks bottles, cans and cartons, crisp packets. Why don't you see things like empty baked bean cans, fish finger packets and washing-up liquid bottles in the street?

5 Find out more about the litter problem. You can get information from the Tidy Britain Group. See page 47 for their address.

The case of the disappearing pack

'The Disappearing Pack' isn't a case for Sherlock Holmes. On the other hand, if the famous detective – or anyone else – could solve the problem, we'd all be a lot happier. The truth is that people *want* litter to disappear.

When materials are returned to nature, that is, allowed to rot into the earth, they are called *biodegradable*. Garden refuse (leaves, flowers, weeds) is a good example. If dumped garden rubbish is allowed to rot in the garden, it is rich in nutrients for the soil.

So people ask 'Why can't packaging rot away and vanish – and so be useful to everyone?'. The fact is that some substances, such as glass and most plastics, are not biodegradable. It is possible to make plastics degrade, but only at the price of losing the properties that make manufacturers choose plastics. Where would we be if plastic bottles started to fall apart in the supermarket or kitchen, before the contents had been used.

The only packaging material that degrades with any speed is paper, and even paper has been known to last for years. Old telephone directories have been dug out of landfill sites in readable condition. Glass doesn't decompose and tinplated steel, aluminium and plastics take years to rot compared with banana skins, for example, which take a few days. But it really does not matter what litter is or how quickly it disappears. The real answer is that people's attitudes to littering have to change.

WHAT YOU CAN DO

Look at the information about the litter left on UK holiday sites, and answer the questions.

1 Compare the figures for 1972 and 1983. Which materials went up and which went down? Say why you think this happened.

2 Now comment on the number of items found on holiday sites for the two years. Again what has gone up and what has gone down? What do you think this is?

3 Carry out your own survey of several streets or open spaces in your area noting the number of pieces of litter you find. What kind of litter is most common? Least common? What conclusions can you draw from your survey?

Source: The British Glass Manufacturers Confederation

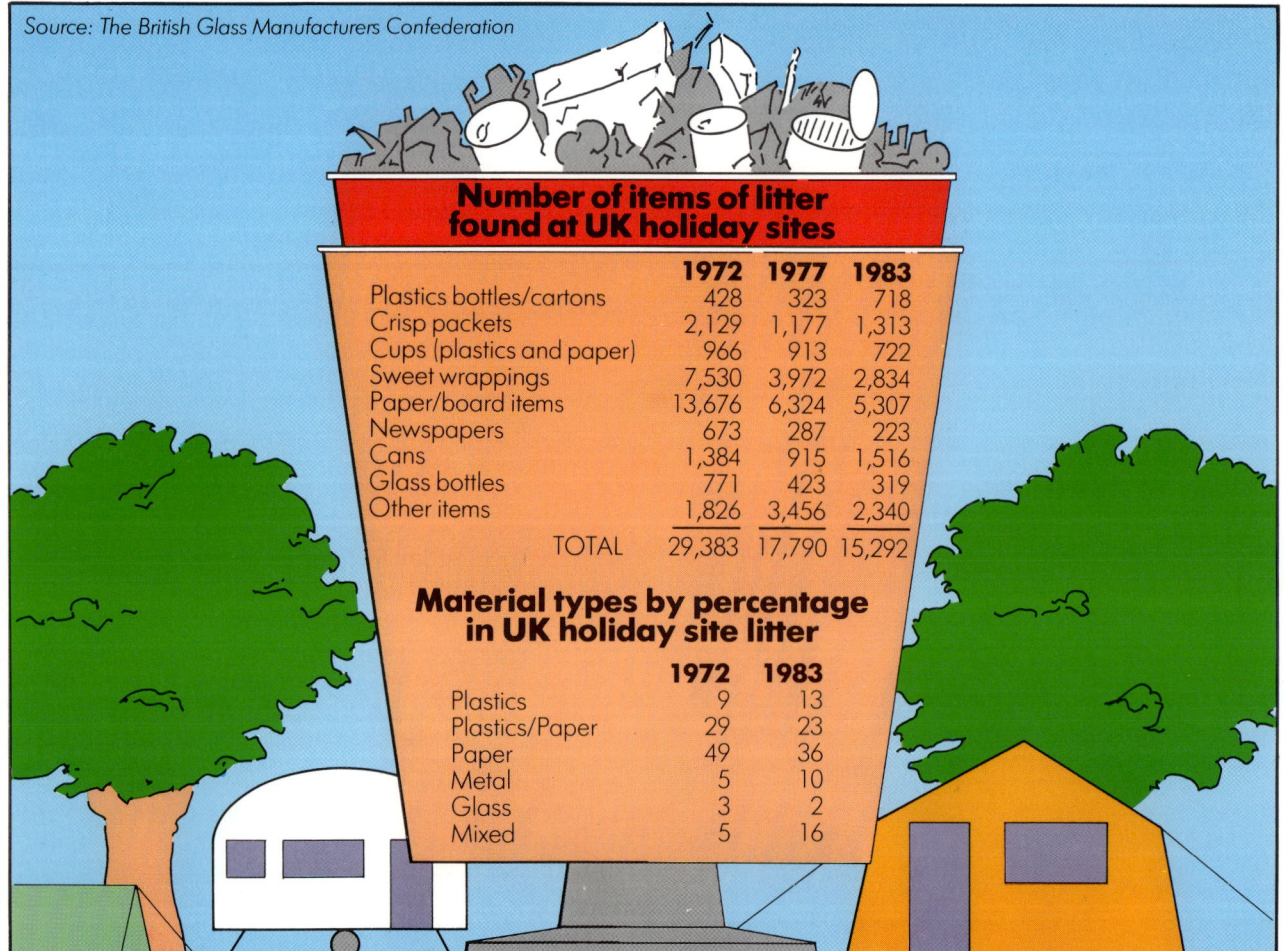

Number of items of litter found at UK holiday sites

	1972	1977	1983
Plastics bottles/cartons	428	323	718
Crisp packets	2,129	1,177	1,313
Cups (plastics and paper)	966	913	722
Sweet wrappings	7,530	3,972	2,834
Paper/board items	13,676	6,324	5,307
Newspapers	673	287	223
Cans	1,384	915	1,516
Glass bottles	771	423	319
Other items	1,826	3,456	2,340
TOTAL	29,383	17,790	15,292

Material types by percentage in UK holiday site litter

	1972	1983
Plastics	9	13
Plastics/Paper	29	23
Paper	49	36
Metal	5	10
Glass	3	2
Mixed	5	16

6 Packaging and the future

WELL, IT LOOKS NICE, BUT WILL THEY LOOK AFTER IT?

WARNING: CONTAINS HUMANS

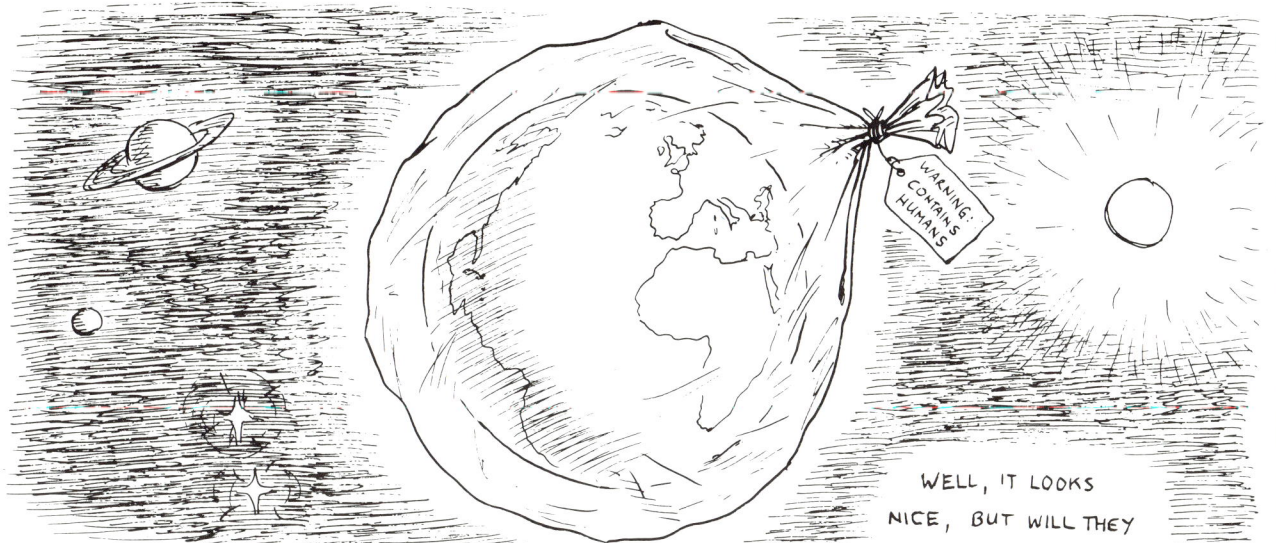

Packaging food is a huge and important industry. Most of us live in towns, we do not have room or time to grow our own food. Today, people want to buy:

1 Food and drinks that are safe, that won't make them ill, and that won't be damaged in transit on the road, by air or by sea.

2 Food that can be stored without deteriorating either in a cupboard, fridge or freezer.

3 A large range of fresh foods that are on sale all year round.

4 'Convenience' or 'ready prepared' foods that can be bought off the shelf in a supermarket.

WHAT YOU CAN DO

1 Suppose you can see into the future, what do you think will happen in 20 years', 50 years', 100 years' time? Will people still want food that is fresh, tasty, nutritious, safe, appetising? Will food have to last for a week, a month, or a year? Discuss in your student group what the future is likely to bring. For example:

● Will there be food rationing because of the increasing world population?

● Will there be more, not less, starvation in the world?

● Will people have to give up fresh food and eat 'prepared' foods?

● Will people's diets change and if so, why and how?

● Some scientists think that in the future food will be packaged in the form of pills, so that people have the right balance of vitamins. What do you think of this idea?

● What problems are there for food packaging companies if these changes actually take place?

2 Having talked about some of the possible problems and the opportunities for the future, describe in your own words what you think will happen – rationing, starvation, foods wars, healthier eating, strict diets, 'live on a pill', or ideas of your own.

3 Suppose you were asked to design the packaging for any one of these – or your own – ideas. Design the pack and explain what's different about it and how it will fit future needs.

Views from the consumer

What do people think about packaging? Consumers don't always agree with the experts.

Here are some views. Do you – or don't you – agree with what's being said? If you were a packaging manufacturer, how would your company overcome each of these problems?

Childproof medicine bottles

'Thank goodness for those tamper-proof pill bottles. They keep the children out of harm's way, although, older people find them very difficult to open.'

Sensibly-shaped containers

'You don't have that many containers to put everything in, so packs should do the whole job themselves. Some things spill in a cupboard, if someone takes something else out. Containers need to be easily stackable and more evenly shaped.'

And sometimes, packaging – food or non-food – can be suitable but just needs a better design:

'I was having trouble yesterday getting some shoelaces out of a bubble on a card . . . having to use scissors you run the risk of cutting the shoelaces.'

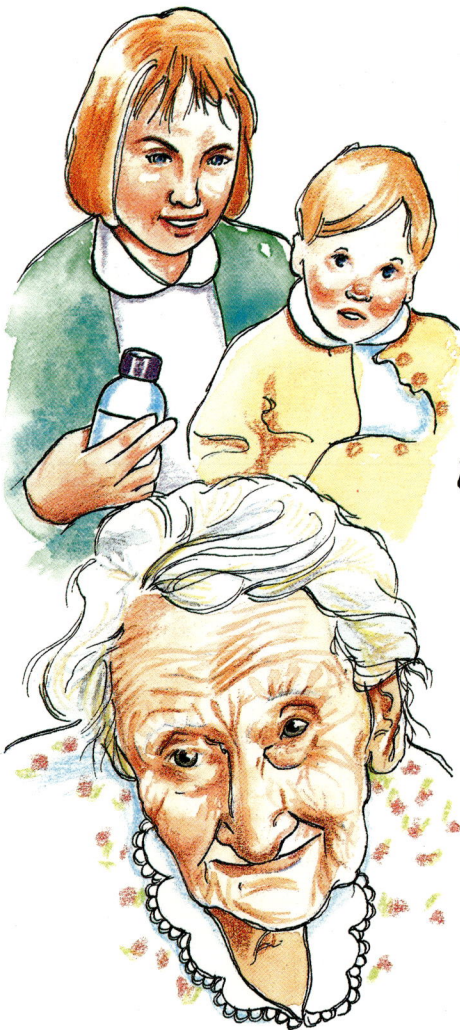

'Those little packs with fruit juice in them, and straws attached to the box are not very rigid and the straws are difficult to get off.'

'I think the cartons and straws are very useful – even the two-year-old can manage those. She puts a straw in it and drinks it quite well. It's nice to be able to buy things that you can just give them.'

Plastic packaged meat and fish

'I think the see-through aspect of plastics with food is good. Especially the things like ham that you buy in plastic containers and you can turn it over and have a look to see how much fat or gristle there is...'

'And also you can see the size of things ... like the number of smoked mackerel in one pack.'

Attractive containers

'I like margarine in plastic containers. You can use it again and again, the tops are more like Tupperware. You can put it on the table and not be embarrassed because they use pretty illustrations.'

Re-usable packaging

'More places should do what the Body Shop do, where you take back your container and get it refilled.'

'You couldn't do that for everything ... it's only in specialised things like make-up and wine ...'

'I think you could do it for most things, like washing-up liquid for instance, but it would obviously take time to set up ...
I wonder if it would be cheaper in the long run ...'

Source: 'Packaging Progress' ICI PLC

Packaging
- protects
- contains
- preserves
- informs
- helps people to choose
- reduces food spoilage
- provides thousands of jobs
- guarantees safety and hygiene
- keeps prices down
- saves energy
- promotes and advertises the product
- helps to stop people tampering with goods
- makes self-service in shops possible

In Britain and throughout the world, packaging means money. In one year, 1986, in the UK alone, £5.3 billion was spent by manufacturers on packaging.

If you didn't know that . . . read on!

A Coca-Cola canning line is able to fill 2,000 cans *a minute!*

Over 60% of all packaging is for FOOD

The packaging of emergency dressings and fluids (such as saline and plasma) saves lives, as in the Falklands War.

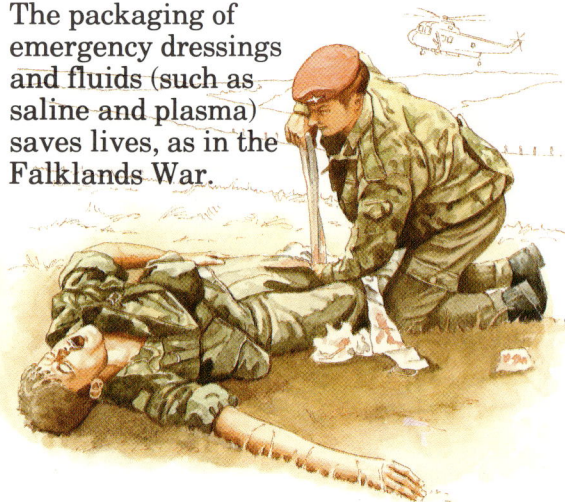

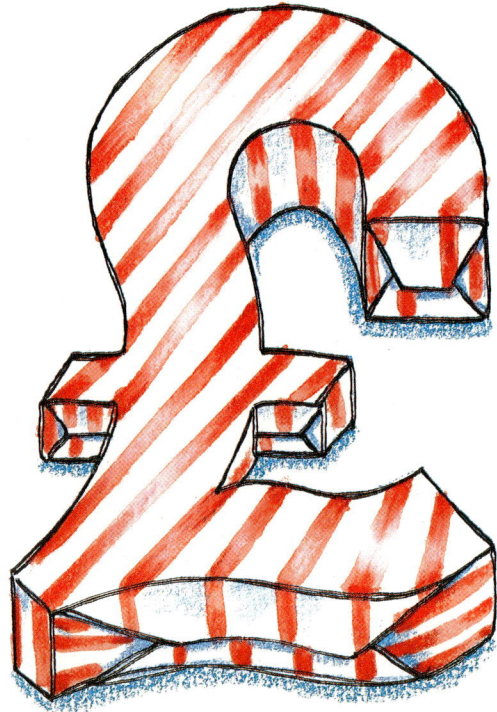

Pizzas made in Britain are specially packaged for sale in Italy and Spain.

A glimpse into the future

The way we live is likely to alter in the next twenty years. How will packaging change to keep up?

Will feeding and eating become different events – will we feed when hungry at home or in convenience restaurants; will we eat gourmet foods at social events?

Will we:
Eat out more – at drive-in restaurants?
Use mail order for all products?
Order by phone, looking at the goods on our TV screens?
Have goods delivered to the door?
All own microwav[illegible] freezers?
All lo[illegible]ment and stop
[illegible]

[illegible]stomer, want:
[illegible] year round?
[illegible]pared food?

[illegible]

a[illegible]
- [illegible]
- [illegible]
- [illegible]

as t[illegible]
- e[illegible]
- st[illegible] and stacking?
- ea[illegible]

as the[illegible]
- full[illegible]

as the [illegible]urer, want:
- bran[illegible] image?
- fast filling lines?
- repeat sales?

as the local authority, want:
- recycling schemes for materials that can sell to cover the costs of the scheme?
- less litter?
- waste without problems?

What does this mean for packaging?

It is likely to mean:

- less material used to package basic foods – combining materials using the least amount of each

- processes to extend the life of food, eg aseptic packaging (at the moment used only for liquid and small particles of food like vegetable bits in soups)

- more modified atmosphere packaging (gases like those we breathe, oxygen, nitrogen and carbon dioxide are put inside the pack) to keep fresh foods longer

- packs which help to brown and crisp food in microwave ovens.

It could also mean:

- mail order goods packaged in basic, undecorated packaging

- there will be fewer shops, as goods are distributed directly from warehouse to homes

- more versatile packaging for use in the freezer, microwave and on the table

- alternative natural resources. In future, oil might be more expensive and not so easy to get out of the ground, and plastics might be made from other vegetable matter.

WHAT YOU CAN DO

The last assignment is a major project which should help you to use the information in this book and develop your skills and knowledge.

Choose any one of these topics:

- changes in packaging technology
- advances in the conservation of resources
- changes in the packaging of (a) food or (b) clothing or (c) other consumer goods
- changes in the use of packaging as a marketing technique.

Find out more about it by writing to packaging firms and research organisations (see the addresses on page 47). Explain the effects that these changes will have in the future, illustrating your work with drawings and pictures.

Glossary

Aerosol A container (metal, plastic or glass) which contains a substance packed under pressure, with a device for releasing it as a fine spray.

Bar coding An international system of small bars or symbols in a pattern that is scanned by a laser beam to identify the product for pricing, stock control and other information.

Biodegradable Decomposable through the action of soil bacteria.

Board Very heavy paper, (over 225gm²), which is often made up of more than one layer.

Celluloid The first plastic, celluloid, was invented in 1869, and was used for billiard balls to avoid using ivory from elephants' tusks.

Chlorofluorocarbons (CFCs) These man-made chemicals are used as propellants in aerosols, as coolants in fridges and air-conditioning plants, as dry-cleaning solvents, in the plastic foam used to make hamburger and other fast-food cartons, in furniture stuffing, and in insulation products.

Consumer A person who uses a product, as opposed to the producer who makes the product. The product can be goods, such as furniture, or services, such as dry-cleaning.

Delicatessen A shop selling prepared delicacies or relishes for the table.

Heat seal A method of joining two or more surfaces by fusion under controlled conditions of temperature, pressure and time, so sealing the contents.

Lamination The bonding of two or more thin layers of plastics, paper or metal. Thin clear plastic foils are often used in laminates to sandwich and protect a printed surface, and/or to improve the protection properties of the package

Land-filling Most waste in the UK is used to fill holes in the ground which have usually been made by quarrying for minerals. Once filled with waste, the holes are turned into leisure areas, such as golf-courses, or sometimes used for agriculture.

Nylon The name given to synthetic plastics made from polyamides. Its main characteristics are elasticity and strength.

Nitrous oxide (NO) This colourless gas is also called laughing gas because it has an exhilarating effect and may even cause laughter. It is popularly known for its use as an anaesthetic or pain-killer during dental or surgical operations, but not so well for its use as a propellant in cream aerosols etc.

Ozone layer The ozone layer, found between 20 and 50 km (12–30 miles) above the earth's surface, screens out 99 per cent of harmful ultraviolet (UV) radiation from the sun. Scientific evidence has shown that the ozone layer is being destroyed by chlorofluorocarbons (CFCs), which are used in a variety of products.

Pack A container (noun). To put material or goods into a container for storage and/or transport (verb).

Pallet A platform or tray for lifting and stacking goods, used with a fork lift truck.

Plant Machinery, equipment.

Plastics Synthetic materials made from organic molecules, such as petroleum (oil). Raw plastics are usually in long chains called polymers and are in granule or powder form. Companies called converters process the raw plastics into the final product, such as bottles or films.

Polymer Plastics raw material usually in granular or powder form.

Recycling The process by which substances are broken down and reconstituted.

Self-service The system by which customers serve themselves with food or goods and pay a cashier, or put money into a machine that then dispenses the goods to them.

Shelf life The length of time that the product remains in a safe and saleable condition under specified conditions of storage.

Shrink wrapping An article is enclosed in a filmy plastic material that shrinks tightly around it.

Standard of living This is the material well-being of a country. It is measured by the average income per head of the population and is used to compare economic development in different countries.

Stratosphere Part of the earth's upper atmosphere. It is about 40 km (25 miles) thick, and contains most of the atmosphere's ozone.

Tinplate Invented by an Englishman, Bryan Donkin, who dipped metal (iron) plates into tin to protect them against rust. He then soldered the plates together into a round container, hence the term, tin-can, which comes from tin-canister.

Addresses

Sources of further information and help (Please send a stamped addressed envelope)

Organisations

Aluminium Federation, Broadway House, Calthorpe Road, Five Ways, Birmingham B15 1TN

British Aerosol Manufacturers Association (BAMA), Kings Buildings, Smith Square, London SW1P 3JJ

British Carton Association, 11 Bedford Row, London WC1

British Fibreboard Packaging Association, Sutherland House, 5–6 Argyll Street, London W1V 1AL

The British Glass Manufacturers Confederation, Northumberland Road, Sheffield S10 2UA

British Paper & Board Industries Federation, Papermakers House, Rivenhall Road, Westlea, Swindon SN5 7BE

British Plastics Federation, 5 Belgrave Square, London SW1X 8PH

British Waste Paper Association, Highgate House, 214 High Street, Guildford, Surrey GU3 1JB

Can Makers Information Service 36 Grosvenor Gardens, London SW1W 0ED

Department of the Environment, Noise, Nuisance and Wastes Division, Romney House, 43 Marsham Street, London SW1P 3PY

Energy Technology Support Unit (ETSU), Building 156, AERE, Harwell, Didcot, Oxon OX11 0RA

INCPEN, The Industry Council for Packaging and the Environment, Premier House, 10 Greycoat Place, London SW1P 1SB

Institute of Wastes Management, 3 Albion Place, Derngate, Northampton NN1 1UD

Liquid Food Carton Manufacturers Association, 30b Wimpole Street, London W1M 8AA

Metal Packaging Manufacturers Association, Elm House, 19 Elmshott Lane, Cippenham, Slough, Berkshire SL1 5QS

National Play Resource Centre, Grumpy House, Vaughan Street, West Gorton, Manchester M12 5DU

The Institute of Packaging, Sysonby Lodge, Nottingham Road, Melton Mowbray, Leicestershire LE13 0NU

Pira, Randalls Road, Leatherhead, Surrey KT22 7RU

The Tidy Britain Group, The Pier, Wigan, Lancashire WN3 4EX

The Warmer Campaign, 83 Mount Ephraim, Tunbridge Wells, Kent TN4 8BS

Warren Spring Laboratory, Gunnelswood Road, Stevenage, Herts

Watford College (for courses in packaging), Hempstead Road, Watford WD1 3EZ

Companies

Coca-Cola Great Britain, Pemberton House, Wrights Lane, London W8 5SN

Coca-Cola & Schweppes Beverages Limited, Charter Place, Uxbridge, Middlesex UB8 1EZ

ICI Chemicals and Polymers, PO Box 90, Wilton, Middlesbrough, Cleveland TS6 8JE

ICI Films, PO Box 6, Shire Park, Bessemer Road, Welwyn Garden City, Herts AL7 1HD

Wimpy International, 10 Windmill Road, London W4 1SD

Useful books

A Handbook of Food Packaging, Frank and Heather Paine, published by Leonard Hill

The World of Plastics, The British Plastics Federation, 5 Belgrave Square, London SW1X 8PH

Magazines

Packaging, 177 Hagden Lane, Watford, Herts WD1 8LN

Packaging News, Maclean Hunter House, Chalk Lane, Cockfosters, Barnet, Herts EN4 0BU

Packaging Week, Benn Ltd, Sovereign Way, Tonbridge, Kent TN9 1RW

Packaging Today, 361 City Road, London EC1V 1LR

Index